Gender Quotas and Women's Representation

Electoral gender quotas have emerged as one of the most critical political reforms of the last two decades, having now been introduced in more than 130 countries worldwide. The recent and global nature of these developments has sparked both scholarly and popular interest in the design, origins, and effects of these policies.

This volume seeks to expand these existing agendas to forge new directions in research on gender quotas and political representation. The topics considered include new paths to adoption, as well as—in the wake of quota introduction—changes in the dynamics of candidate selection, the status and role of women in legislative institutions, and the impact that women have on policy-making. Expanding the scope of quota studies, the contributions also address trends in different political parties and different levels of government, the effectiveness of quotas in democratic and non-democratic settings, and whether there might be non-quota mechanisms that could be pursued together with, or in lieu of, gender quotas in order to increase women's political representation.

This book was originally published as a special issue of *Representation*.

Mona Lena Krook is an Associate Professor of Political Science at Rutgers University, New Jersey, USA. She is the author of *Quotas for Women in Politics: Gender and Candidate Selection Reform Worldwide* (2009) and co-editor of *The Impact of Gender Quotas* (2012).

Pär Zetterberg is a Researcher in the Department of Government at Uppsala University, Sweden. His research focuses on political recruitment and political representation in comparative perspective, especially in Latin America, with a particular emphasis on the potential for gender quotas to remedy inequalities in politics.

Gender Quotas and Women's Representation

New directions in research

Edited by
Mona Lena Krook and Pär Zetterberg

Routledge
Taylor & Francis Group

LONDON AND NEW YORK

First published 2016
by Routledge
2 Park Square, Milton Park, Abingdon, Oxon, OX14 4RN, UK

and by Routledge
711 Third Avenue, New York, NY 10017, USA

Routledge is an imprint of the Taylor & Francis Group, an informa business

British Library Cataloguing in Publication Data
A catalogue record for this book is available from the British Library

ISBN 13: 978-1-138-90742-3

Typeset in Frutiger
by RefineCatch Limited, Bungay, Suffolk

Publisher's Note
The publisher accepts responsibility for any inconsistencies that may have arisen during the conversion of this book from journal articles to book chapters, namely the possible inclusion of journal terminology.

Disclaimer
Every effort has been made to contact copyright holders for their permission to reprint material in this book. The publishers would be grateful to hear from any copyright holder who is not here acknowledged and will undertake to rectify any errors or omissions in future editions of this book.

Contents

Citation Information

The chapters in this book were originally published in *Representation*, volume 50, issue 3 (September 2014). When citing this material, please use the original page numbering for each article, as follows:

Chapter 1
Introduction: Gender Quotas and Women's Representation—New Directions in Research
Mona Lena Krook and Pär Zetterberg
Representation, volume 50, issue 3 (September 2014) pp. 287–294

Chapter 2
Quota Adoption and the Exogenous Track Model: The Parity Laws in the French Pacific Collectivities
Kerryn Baker
Representation, volume 50, issue 3 (September 2014) pp. 295–306

Chapter 3
Why are Representational Guarantees Adopted for Women and Minorities? Comparing Constituency Formation and Electoral Quota Design within Countries
Elin Bjarnegård and Pär Zetterberg
Representation, volume 50, issue 3 (September 2014) pp. 307–320

Chapter 4
Federalism and Gender Quotas in Mexico: Analysing Propietario *and* Suplente *Nominations*
Fernanda Vidal Correa
Representation, volume 50, issue 3 (September 2014) pp. 321–335

Chapter 5
Gender Quotas and 'Women-Friendly' Candidate Selection: Evidence from Belgium
Audrey Vandeleene
Representation, volume 50, issue 3 (September 2014) pp. 337–349

Chapter 6

The Effectiveness of Quotas: Vertical and Horizontal Discrimination in Spain
Pablo Oñate
Representation, volume 50, issue 3 (September 2014) pp. 351–364

Chapter 7

Tracing Gender Differences in Parliamentary Debates: A Growth Curve Analysis of Ugandan MPs' Activity Levels in Plenary Sessions, 1998–2008
Vibeke Wang
Representation, volume 50, issue 3 (September 2014) pp. 365–377

Chapter 8

Present without Presence? Gender, Quotas and Debate Recognition in the Ugandan Parliament
Amanda Clayton, Cecilia Josefsson and Vibeke Wang
Representation, volume 50, issue 3 (September 2014) pp. 379–392

Chapter 9

Alternatives to Gender Quotas: Electoral Financing of Women Candidates in Malawi
Happy M. Kayuni and Ragnhild L. Muriaas
Representation, volume 50, issue 3 (September 2014) pp. 393–404

For any permission-related enquiries please visit:
http://www.tandfonline.com/page/help/permissions

Notes on Contributors

Kerryn Baker is a PhD scholar in the State Society and Governance in Melanesia Program at the Australian National University, Canberra, Australia.

Elin Bjarnegård is an Assistant Professor in the Department of Government at Uppsala University, Sweden. Her research interests are within the field of comparative politics, with a particular focus on gender, masculinities, political recruitment, and peace and conflict. Her work has been published in journals such as *International Interactions* and *Foreign Affairs*, and her book entitled *Gender, Informal Institutions and Political Recruitment* was published in 2013.

Amanda Clayton is a PhD candidate in the Department of Political Science at the University of Washington, Seattle, Washington, USA. During the 2014/2015 academic year, she will be a Postdoctoral Fellow at the Free University of Berlin, Germany, as well as hold a Research Fellowship at the Women and Public Policy Program at Harvard Kennedy School, Cambridge, Massachusetts, USA.

Cecilia Josefsson is a PhD candidate in the Department of Government at Uppsala University, Sweden. She also currently holds a research scholarship at the Swedish Parliament.

Happy M. Kayuni is an Associate Professor in the Political and Administrative Studies Department at the University of Malawi, Zomba, Malawi. He is currently completing a PhD in Political Science at the University of Western Cape, Cape Town, South Africa. He previously worked as Programme Manager for Women's World Banking-Malawi Affiliate. His research and publications address public administration/management, gender, development, international relations, and party politics.

Mona Lena Krook is an Associate Professor of Political Science at Rutgers University, New Brunswick, New Jersey, USA. She is the author of *Quotas for Women in Politics: Gender and Candidate Selection Reform Worldwide* (2009) and co-editor of *The Impact of Gender Quotas* (2012), exploring the impact of quotas beyond numbers in Western Europe, Latin America, Asia/the Middle East and Sub-Saharan Africa. Her recent work also examines 'non-quota' strategies to promote women in politics.

Ragnhild L. Muriaas is an Associate Professor in the Department of Comparative Politics at the University of Bergen, Norway. She has published extensively on questions related to women's representation, political decentralisation, and traditional institutions in Southern and Eastern Africa. Her work has appeared in *The Journal of Contemporary African Studies, Government and Opposition, Democratization, Women's Studies International Forum*, and *The Journal of Modern African Studies*. She is the editor-in-chief of *Norsk Statsvitenskapelig Tidsskrift* (the Norwegian Journal of Political Science).

Pablo Oñate is a Professor of Political Science at the University of Valencia, Spain. He has published on legislatures, political elites, political parties, and party systems. His current research project analyses conceptions of political representation among citizens and MPs.

Audrey Vandeleene is a PhD candidate at the Institute of Political Science Louvain-Europe, Université catholique de Louvain, Belgium. Her research interests cover party politics, candidate selection, intra-party democracy, electoral systems, and women-in-politics.

Fernanda Vidal Correa is a Fellow at the Institute of Legal Research, National Autonomous University of Mexico, Mexico City, Mexico. She is the author of several publications on women in politics in Mexico, including the impact of the decentralisation of party candidate selection processes and renewed federalism on women's representation in state congresses. Her current research focuses on intra-party nominations, gender studies, and party members' political rights.

Vibeke Wang is currently working on a three-year post-doctoral project at the Chr. Michelsen Institute, Bergen, Norway.

Pär Zetterberg is a Researcher in the Department of Government at Uppsala University, Sweden. His research interests include candidate recruitment and political representation in comparative perspective, with particular focus on electoral gender quotas. He has published his research in journals such as *Political Research Quarterly, Parliamentary Affairs, Development and Change*, and *Politics & Gender*.

INTRODUCTION: GENDER QUOTAS AND WOMEN'S REPRESENTATION—NEW DIRECTIONS IN RESEARCH

Mona Lena Krook and Pär Zetterberg

This article introduces the special issue and places the contributions in context. It begins with a brief discussion of main trends in quota research to date, focusing on major findings in relation to gender quotas and women's political representation. It then presents an overview of the articles in the special issue, detailing their research strategies and theoretical and empirical findings. The final part of the section addresses the implications of these studies – and work on gender quotas more generally – for forging new research agendas on political representation.

Electoral gender quotas have emerged as one of the critical political reforms of the last two decades, having now been introduced in more than 130 countries worldwide (Krook 2009).[1] While the majority of these provisions have been adopted by individual political parties, a significant and growing proportion involve changes to constitutions or electoral laws requiring that all parties select a certain percentage of female candidates. The recent and global nature of these developments has sparked both scholarly and popular interest in gender quota designs, origins and effects (Dahlerup 2006; Krook 2009; Tremblay 2008). The result has been the consolidation of a broad body of knowledge on the origins and technical aspects of quota implementation, highlighting the actors mobilising for quota reform in various countries (Anderson and Swiss 2014; Bush 2011; Krook 2006) and the factors shaping the effectiveness of quotas in increasing the numbers of women elected (Jones 2009; Krook 2009; Paxton et al. 2010; Schwindt-Bayer 2009; Tripp and Kang 2008). This has led to widespread recognition by international actors of the role of well-devised gender quotas in spurring the dramatic jumps witnessed in recent years in terms of the proportions of women elected to national parliaments around the globe (Inter-Parliamentary Union 2013), even if not all countries at the top of this list apply formal quota policies (Krook 2014).

A new wave of quota research takes this work forward by observing that quotas are not simply about increasing the numbers of women elected (Franceschet et al. 2012; Krook and Messing-Mathie 2013; Zetterberg 2009b). Inspired by competing claims put forward during debates for quota adoption, this 'second generation' of quota research largely focuses on the implications of quotas for a wide variety of representative processes. In terms of descriptive representation, scholars explore what kinds of women are elected as a result of quota policies, finding that 'quota women' are often as—and sometimes even more—qualified as their non-quota counterparts, both male and female (Josefsson 2014; Murray 2010; O'Brien 2012; Sater 2012), while also enhancing diversity in legislator backgrounds (Bird 2003; Franceschet and

Piscopo 2012; Hughes 2011), even if gendered norms of recruitment continue to circumscribe women's political careers (Franceschet and Piscopo 2014).

With regard to substantive representation, studies ask whether an increase in the numbers of women elected as a result of gender quotas leads to greater attention to women's issues in the policy-making process. Evidence from a diverse range of countries provides mixed conclusions. Some studies find a clear impact on policy discourses and outcomes (Barnes 2012; Bauer and Burnet 2013; Childs 2004; Wang 2013; Xydias 2007; Yoon 2011), while others observe that quotas do not appear to eliminate all barriers to the articulation of women's concerns (Larson 2012; Tønnessen and al-Nagar 2013; Zetterberg 2008). In a seminal article, Franceschet and Piscopo (2008) argue that these distinct patterns may be due in part to contradictory pressures on women elected through quotas, requiring them to navigate between a 'mandate effect', a feeling of obligation to act on behalf of women, and a 'label effect', a sense of stigma associated with their mode of election leading them to be apprehensive about advocating for the rights of women (cf. Childs and Krook 2012).

A final group of analyses considers the impact of quotas on symbolic representation, posing a variety of creative questions regarding the potential transformative nature of gender quotas—on women, politics, or society more generally. Some of this work gauges whether the introduction of gender quotas has created sustainable gains in women's representation that would endure if quotas were withdrawn (Bhavnani 2009; Darhour and Dahlerup 2014)—or, alternatively, whether quota adoption has produced a spillover effect increasing women's nomination and election in political offices not governed by quota regulations (Davidson-Schmich 2010; Shin 2014). Related research maps whether quotas for women in politics inspire the introduction of quotas in other spheres, for example on corporate boards (Franceschet and Piscopo 2013; Meier 2014). Other work examines what quotas have meant in terms of women's political engagement (Zetterberg 2009a) and women's empowerment more broadly, whether inside political parties (Verge and de la Fuente 2014), within society (Beaman et al. 2009, 2012), or inside the home (Burnet 2011).

The contributions to this special issue seek to expand these research agendas further, taking the quota literature in a variety of new directions and presenting novel approaches to the study of political representation. The topics taken up include additional paths to quota adoption, as well as—in the wake of quota introduction—changes (or not) to existing dynamics of candidate selection and the status and role of women in legislative institutions. Expanding the scope of quota studies, the articles also address trends across different political parties and levels of government, as well as the effectiveness of quotas in democratic and non-democratic settings. The final, more critical article raises questions as to whether there may be non-quota mechanisms that could be pursued together with, or in lieu of, gender quotas to increase women's political representation.

The first two articles address the introduction of gender quotas, expanding the focus to new contexts and in relation to other social groups. The contribution by Kerryn Baker considers how the implementation of the French parity laws in the French Pacific collectivities fits in with established discourses of quota adoption. Calling into question assumptions that quotas by definition represent an 'exogenous shock' to the political system, she proposes a theoretical distinction between endogenous and exogenous tracks to quota introduction. She signals how the French parity law stretches beyond the borders of mainland France, and thereby is imposed from the outside rather than developing internally within the local political system. For this reason, however, these islands constitute outliers within the Pacific region, which has the lowest average level of female political representation in the world.[2]

Elin Bjarnegård and Pär Zetterberg also take up the issue of quota adoption, but focus on states where quotas exist for both women and minority groups, comparing similarities and differences across these policies. Going beyond work mapping the presence of quotas for women and minorities (Hughes 2011; Krook and O'Brien 2010), they qualify the concept of 'quota types' by focusing on whether the quota implies the creation of a special constituency. Their analysis reveals substantial differences in the philosophy behind quotas for these two groups. Minorities tend to be guaranteed representation via the creation of special constituencies, whereas gender quotas more commonly imply integration into pre-existing constituencies (cf. Bird 2014; Htun 2004). The authors conclude on this basis that gender quotas and quotas for minorities seem to rest on somewhat different underlying normative motives.

The next two contributions tackle new questions related to gender quota implementation. The focus of Fernanda Vidal Correa's article is the application of quota laws in a sample of 12 Mexican states, highlighting two aspects of policy design that become apparent when bringing the analysis down to the subnational level, which has been thus far been understudied in the quota literature (but see dos Santos 2012; Jones 1998; Zetterberg 2008). Using data on the nomination and election of women in these states between 1998 and 2010, she observes that quota impact at the subnational levels depends on the design of state-level laws. In Mexico, as she points out, some state quota laws dictate only partial or no enforcement at all. Further, the two-nominee system—whereby the first person runs for the seat (*propietario*) while the second is elected as a substitute (*suplente*)—provides opportunities for parties to circumvent the spirit of the law. Quotas in some states may apply only to *suplentes*, resulting in women's entrapment in substitute and thus powerless positions. Vidal Correa therefore highlights the need to move the analysis down to the subnational level, while also examining who in fact is promoted through the quota policy.

Audrey Vandeleene, in comparison, explores how quotas may—or may not—lead to changes in candidate selection processes in ways that are more 'women-friendly' (see Reiser 2014 for comparisons among women and other groups). She approaches this question in a slightly different way than Bjarnegård and Zetterberg (2011), who theorise what types of quotas may have the most lasting impact in terms of changing candidate selection procedures in a more permanent fashion, such that women would still be nominated and elected even if quotas were withdrawn. In the article, Vandeleene collects data from party statutes and interviews to map differences across the main political parties in Belgium in terms of who selects candidates and how the selection process is organised, with the goal being to gauge whether quotas lead to substantive changes in decision-making procedures. She uncovers substantial variations across political parties, highlighting what reforms are necessary in order to open up candidate selection procedures to women's increased participation.

The following three articles address patterns stemming from gender quota implementation that may signal the broader impact—or not—of quota reforms, particularly with regard to women's status and role in legislative institutions. The contribution by Pablo Oñate tracks whether the application of gender quotas has eroded traditional structures of vertical and horizontal discrimination in the political sphere, whereby women are excluded from leadership positions and allocated to committees dealing with 'feminine' policy concerns, using data from the national congress and 17 subnational legislatures in Spain. Echoing the findings of Verge and de la Fuente (2014), who discover very little transformation in gendered structures within Spanish political parties, Oñate observes that the gender parity law has not altered differential access for women and men to these positions and committees, despite substantial numbers of women in these legislative bodies (cf. Towns 2003).

Vibeke Wang approaches this question from a different angle, examining whether being elected through reserved seats has led female members of parliament (MPs) in Uganda to be less active than non-quota legislators, given widespread expectations that quota women will be more pliable, strongly beholden to party leaders, and act as subordinate or 'token' representatives (cf. Goetz and Hassim 2003). Drawing on a unique dataset, she tests this hypothesis with a hierarchical growth curve analysis of MPs' activity levels in the plenary proceedings in the national assembly from 1998 to 2008. She finds that in fact there are no significant differences among women in terms of their activity levels. Indeed, the contrary is true: overall, women are as active as men in plenary debates, with female MPs holding leadership positions speaking consistently more than any other group. As such, quota women are not inactive or invisible in decision-making processes.

In a separate analysis of Uganda, Amanda Clayton, Cecilia Josefsson, and Vibeke Wang investigate whether female MPs in general, and women elected via quotas in particular, are accorded respect and authority in parliament. They operationalise this question in terms of parliamentary recognition, or the number of times an individual MP is referred to by name in plenary debates, using data from 2001 to 2008. Taking into account other possible determinants of MP recognition, they find that women elected to reserved seats are significantly less recognised over time when compared to men and women in open seats. Juxtaposed with the findings of the previous article, this suggests that there may not be any differences in legislative behaviour, in terms of speaking, but that quota women are not treated on par with other MPs. This recalls the 'label effect' theorised by Franceschet and Piscopo (2008), whereby women elected via quotas may be stigmatised in other ways stemming from their mode of election.

The final article by Happy M. Kayuni and Ragnhild L. Muriaas strikes a more sceptical note, pointing out that gender quotas represent only one solution to women's underrepresentation in politics. More specifically, in relation to the well-known 'supply and demand' model of candidate selection (cf. Norris and Lovenduski 1995), quotas reflect a demand-side solution—overlooking potential supply-side interventions that could help make women stronger candidates (but see Krook and Norris 2014). To this end, they analyse the '50-50 campaign' organised in the run-up to the 2009 elections in Malawi, which equipped women with financial resources and publicity to support their political campaigns. Although women's representation increased notably in these elections, Kayuni and Muriaas conclude that even with electoral financing assistance, party organisations remained biased and weakly committed to the promotion of female candidates—even as women demonstrated that they could win elections.

In mapping new frontiers for gender quota research, the articles in this special issue contribute to concept formation by rethinking what quotas are and what they do; theory development by nuancing how far quotas can go in terms of re-gendering the political sphere; methodological sophistication by parsing out the effects of 'quotas' versus those attributable to 'sex' or 'gender' in terms of quota impact; and comparative analysis by expanding the scope of study to include quotas for other groups and non-quota strategies for empowering women in politics.[3] Even in a now well-established literature, which has begun to be incorporated into the work of non-gender scholars (see Krook and Messing-Mathie 2013), these studies signal that there are still many important research questions yet to be asked and answered with regard to gender quotas and dynamics of political representation.

ACKNOWLEDGEMENTS

The articles in this special issue originated in the 'Electoral Quotas and Political Representation: Comparative Perspectives' workshop organised as part of the European Consortium for Political Research Joint Sessions of Workshops in Mainz, Germany, in March 2013. Mona Lena Krook received financial support from the National Science Foundation's Early Career Development Program (SES-1341129). Pär Zetterberg's contribution was supported by the *Riksbankens Jubileumsfond* (dnr 421-2010-1638).

NOTES

1. For an updated list, see http://www.quotaproject.org.
2. See http://www.ipu.org/wmn-e/world.htm.
3. On the issue of gender quotas and comparison, see the special issues on 'Electoral Quotas and Political Representation: Comparative Perspectives', in *International Political Science Review* 35 (1): 3–118, and 'Gender Quotas and Comparative Politics', in *Politics & Gender* 9 (3): 299–328.

References

ANDERSON, MIRIAM J. and LIAM SWISS. 2014. Peace accords and the adoption of electoral quotas for women in the developing world, 1990–2006. *Politics & Gender* 10 (1): 33–61.

BARNES, TIFFANY D. 2012. Gender and legislative preferences: evidence from the Argentine provinces. *Politics & Gender* 8 (4): 483–507.

BAUER, GRETCHEN and JENNIE E. BURNET. 2013. Gender quotas, democracy, and women's representation in Africa: some insights from democratic Botswana and autocratic Rwanda. *Women's Studies International Forum* 41 (2): 103–12.

BEAMAN, LORI, RAGHABENDRA CHATTOPADHYAY, ROHINI PANDE and PETIA TOPALOVA. 2009. Powerful women: does exposure reduce bias? *Quarterly Journal of Economics* 124 (4): 1497–540.

BEAMAN, LORI, ESTHER DUFLO, ROHINI PANDE and PETIA TOPALOVA. 2012. Female leadership raises aspirations and educational attainment for girls: a policy experiment in India. *Science* 335 (6068): 582–6.

BHAVNANI, RIKHIL R. 2009. Do electoral quotas work after they are withdrawn? Evidence from a natural experiment in India. *American Political Science Review* 103 (1): 23–35.

BIRD, KAREN. 2003. Who are the women? Where are the women? And what difference can they make? Effects of gender parity in French municipal elections. *French Politics* 1 (1): 5–38.

BIRD, KAREN. 2014. Ethnic quotas and ethnic representation worldwide. *International Political Science Review* 35 (1): 12–26.

BJARNEGÅRD, ELIN and PÄR ZETTERBERG. 2011. Removing quotas, maintaining representation: overcoming gender inequalities in political party recruitment. *Representation* 47 (2): 187–99.

BURNET, JENNIE E. 2011. Women have found respect: gender quotas, symbolic representation, and female empowerment in Rwanda. *Politics & Gender* 7 (3): 303–34.

BUSH, SARAH SUNN. 2011. International politics and the spread of quotas for women in legislatures. *International Organization* 65 (1): 103–37.

CHILDS, SARAH. 2004. *New Labour's Women MPs: Women Representing Women*. London: Routledge.

CHILDS, SARAH and MONA LENA KROOK. 2012. Labels and mandates in the United Kingdom. In *The Impact of Gender Quotas*, edited by Susan Franceschet, Mona Lena Krook and Jennifer M. Piscopo. New York: Oxford University Press, pp. 89–102.

DAHLERUP, DRUDE (ed.). 2006. *Women, Quotas, and Politics*. New York: Routledge.

DARHOUR, HANANE and DRUDE DAHLERUP. 2014. Sustainable representation of women through gender quotas: a decade's experience in Morocco. *Women's Studies International Forum* 41 (2): 132–42.

DAVIDSON-SCHMICH, LOUISE K. 2010. Gender quota compliance and contagion in the 2009 Bundestag election. *German Politics & Society* 28 (3): 133–55.

DOS SANTOS, PEDRO G. 2012. Gendering representation: parties, institutions, and the under-representation of women in Brazil's state legislatures. PhD Diss., University of Kansas.

FRANCESCHET, SUSAN and JENNIFER M. PISCOPO. 2008. Gender quotas and women's substantive representation: lessons from Argentina. *Politics & Gender* 4 (3): 393–425.

FRANCESCHET, SUSAN and JENNIFER M. PISCOPO. 2012. Gender and political backgrounds in Argentina. In *The Impact of Gender Quotas*, edited by Susan Franceschet, Mona Lena Krook and Jennifer M. Piscopo. New York: Oxford University Press, pp. 43–56.

FRANCESCHET, SUSAN and JENNIFER M. PISCOPO. 2013. Equality, democracy, and the broadening and deepening of gender quotas. *Politics & Gender* 9 (3): 310–16.

FRANCESCHET, SUSAN and JENNIFER M. PISCOPO. 2014. Sustaining gendered practices? Power, parties, and elite political networks in Argentina. *Comparative Political Studies* 47 (1): 85–110.

FRANCESCHET, SUSAN, MONA LENA KROOK and JENNIFER M. PISCOPO (eds). 2012. *The Impact of Gender Quotas*. New York: Oxford University Press.

GOETZ, ANNE-MARIE and SHIREEN HASSIM (eds). 2003. *No Shortcuts to Power: African Women in Politics and Policy Making*. London: Zed Books.

HTUN, MALA. 2004. Is gender like ethnicity? The political representation of identity groups. *Perspectives on Politics* 2 (3): 439–58.

HUGHES, MELANIE M. 2011. Intersectionality, quotas, and minority women's political representation worldwide. *American Political Science Review* 105 (3): 604–20.

INTER-PARLIAMENTARY UNION. 2013. *Women in Parliament in 2012: The Year in Perspective*, available at http://www.ipu.org/PDF/publications/WIP2012E.pdf (accessed 19 June 2014).

JONES, MARK P. 1998. Gender quotas, electoral laws, and the election of women: lessons from the Argentine provinces. *Comparative Political Studies* 31 (1): 3–21.

JONES, MARK P. 2009. Gender quotas, electoral laws, and the election of women: evidence from the Latin American vanguard. *Comparative Political Studies* 42 (1): 56–81.

JOSEFSSON, CECILIA. 2014. Who benefits from gender quotas? Assessing the impact of election procedure reform on Members of Parliament's attributes in Uganda. *International Political Science Review* 35 (1): 93–105.

KROOK, MONA LENA. 2006. Reforming representation: the diffusion of candidate gender quotas worldwide. *Politics & Gender* 2 (3): 303–27.

KROOK, MONA LENA. 2009. *Quotas for Women in Politics: Gender and Candidate Selection Reform Worldwide*. New York: Oxford University Press.

KROOK, MONA LENA. 2014. Electoral gender quotas: a conceptual analysis. *Comparative Political Studies* 47 (9): 1268–93.

KROOK, MONA LENA and ANDREA MESSING-MATHIE. 2013. Gender quotas and comparative politics: past, present, and future research agendas. *Politics & Gender* 9 (3): 299–303.

KROOK, MONA and PIPPA NORRIS. 2014. Beyond quotas: strategies to promote gender equality in elected office. *Political Studies* 62 (1): 2–20.

KROOK, MONA LENA and DIANA Z. O'BRIEN. 2010. The politics of group representation: quotas for women and minorities worldwide. *Comparative Politics* 42 (3): 253–72.

LARSON, ANNA. 2012. Collective identities, institutions, security, and state building in Afghanistan. In *The Impact of Gender Quotas*, edited by Susan Franceschet, Mona Lena Krook and Jennifer M. Piscopo. New York: Oxford University Press, pp. 136–53.

MEIER, PETRA. 2014. Quotas for advisory committees, business and politics: just more of the same? *International Political Science Review* 35 (1): 106–18.

MURRAY, RAINBOW. 2010. Second among unequals? A study of whether France's 'quota women' are up to the job. *Politics & Gender* 6 (1): 93–118.

NORRIS, P. and JONI LOVENDUSKI. 1995. *Political Recruitment: Gender, Race and Class in the British Parliament*. New York: Cambridge University Press.

O'BRIEN, DIANA Z. 2012. Quotas and qualifications in Uganda. In *The Impact of Gender Quotas*, edited by Susan Franceschet, Mona Lena Krook and Jennifer M. Piscopo. New York: Oxford University Press, pp. 57–71.

PAXTON, PAMELA, MELANIE M. HUGHES and MATTHEW A. PAINTER. 2010. Growth in women's political representation: a longitudinal exploration of democracy, electoral system and gender quotas. *European Journal of Political Research* 49 (1): 25–52.

REISER, MARION. 2014. The universe of group representation in Germany: analysing formal and informal party rules and quotas in the process of candidate selection. *International Political Science Review* 35 (1): 55–66.

SATER, JAMES N. 2012. Reserved seats, patriarchy, and patronage in Morocco. In *The Impact of Gender Quotas*, edited by Susan Franceschet, Mona Lena Krook and Jennifer M. Piscopo. New York: Oxford University Press, pp. 57–71.

SCHWINDT-BAYER, LESLIE A. 2009. Making quotas work: the effect of gender quota laws on the election of women. *Legislative Studies Quarterly* 34 (1): 5–28.

SHIN, KI-YOUNG. 2014. Women's sustainable representation and the spillover effect of electoral gender quotas in South Korea. *International Political Science Review* 35 (1): 80–92.

TØNNESSEN, LIV and SAMIA AL-NAGAR. 2013. The women's quota in conflict ridden Sudan: ideological battles for and against gender equality. *Women's Studies International Forum* 41 (2): 122–31.

TOWNS, ANN. 2003. Understanding the effects of larger ratios of women in national legislatures: proportions and gender differentiation in Sweden and Norway. *Women & Politics* 25 (1–2): 1–29.

TREMBLAY, MANON (ed.). 2008. *Women and Legislative Representation: Electoral Systems, Political Parties, and Sex Quotas*. New York: Palgrave.

TRIPP, AILI MARI and ALICE KANG. 2008. The global impact of quotas on the fast track to increased female legislative representation. *Comparative Political Studies* 41 (3): 338–61.

VERGE, TÀNIA and MARIA DE LA FUENTE. 2014. Playing with different cards: party politics, gender quotas and women's empowerment. *International Political Science Review* 35 (1): 67–79.

WANG, VIBEKE. 2013. Women changing policy outcomes: learning from pro-women legislation in the Ugandan parliament. *Women's Studies International Forum* 41 (2): 113–21.

XYDIAS, CHRISTINA V. 2007. Inviting more women to the party: gender quotas and women's substantive representation in Germany. *International Journal of Sociology* 37 (4): 52–66.

YOON, MI YUNG. 2011. More women in the Tanzanian legislature: do numbers matter? *Journal of Contemporary African Studies* 29 (1): 83–98.

ZETTERBERG, PÄR. 2008. The downside of gender quotas? Institutional constraints on women in Mexican state legislatures. *Parliamentary Affairs* 61 (3): 442–60.

ZETTERBERG, PÄR. 2009a. Do gender quotas foster women's political engagement? Lessons from Latin America. *Political Research Quarterly* 62 (4): 715–30.

ZETTERBERG, PÄR. 2009b. Engineering equality? Assessing the multiple impacts of electoral gender quotas. PhD Diss., Uppsala University.

QUOTA ADOPTION AND THE EXOGENOUS TRACK MODEL: THE PARITY LAWS IN THE FRENCH PACIFIC COLLECTIVITIES

Kerryn Baker

Drawing on the work of Dahlerup and Freidenvall (2005), this article considers how the implementation of the French parity laws in the Pacific collectivities fits in with established discourses of quota adoption. It proposes that there is another axis of quota adoption—the 'exogenous' and 'endogenous' track models. In France, the parity laws, introduced in 1999, have had mixed results, with a large increase of women councillors at municipal level, significant changes at regional and European levels, but a disappointing impact on the gender make-up of the National Assembly. The impact of the parity laws, however, stretches well beyond the borders of mainland France. While the Pacific region has one of the lowest levels of women's representation in the world, the parity laws have dramatically increased the number of female legislators in the French territories. The introduction of the parity laws in the French Pacific territories constitutes an example of 'exogenous' track quota adoption, in which quotas can truly be defined as exogenous shocks to the local political systems.

Introduction

France introduced two constitutional amendments known as the parity laws in 1999, mandating that political parties put forward equal numbers of male and female candidates. In France, the parity laws have had mixed results, with a large increase of women councillors at the municipal level, significant changes at regional and European levels, but a disappointing impact on the gender make-up of the National Assembly (Murray 2008). France currently has 26.2% women's representation in its National Assembly, and 22.5% in the Senate (IPU 2014).

The parity laws were also implemented in the overseas departments and collectivities of the realm of France. This includes three collectivities in the Pacific Islands region: New Caledonia, French Polynesia, and Wallis and Futuna. In contrast to the experiences of quota implementation in the French National Assembly, the implementation of the parity laws in the legislatures of the French Pacific collectivities has been described as 'a real success' (SPC 2007). While the Pacific Islands region has one of the lowest levels of women's representation in the world, the parity laws have dramatically increased the number of female legislators in the French territories. More than half of the legislators in the French Polynesian Assembly are women, and women's representation in the New Caledonian Congress stands at over 40%. The effects of the parity law have been less pronounced in the territory of Wallis and

Futuna. Nevertheless, while its level of women's representation, at 20%, is lower than the other French collectivities, it is still significantly higher than most other Pacific states and territories, where the average level of women's representation is 5.5%.[1]

In this article, I challenge the idea in existing literature on quota adoption that quotas in all cases constitute an 'exogenous shock' to a political system, arguing that many quotas could be considered endogenous developments as they are adopted by the political institutions in which they will be implemented. Seeking to take quota adoption research in a new direction, I propose that in addition to the two models set out by Dahlerup and Freidenvall (2005)—the 'fast' and 'incremental' tracks—there is another axis of quota adoption, contrasting 'exogenous' and 'endogenous' tracks. The 'exogenous' track model relates to quota adoption in cases where a quota policy is not adopted by a political institution but instead imposed upon it from the outside, for example in a colonial context, or as a result of post-conflict reconstruction of political institutions. I illustrate these dynamics through a case study of the French Pacific, situating the implementation of parity in these territories with patterns in the mainland.

The Exogenous/Endogenous Quota Adoption Axis

The two commonly used quota development narratives are those defined by Dahlerup and Freidenvall (2005) as the 'fast' track and the 'incremental' track. They distinguish between quota adoption as a method to rapidly increase women's participation in decision-making bodies from a low base level of representation—the fast track—and quota adoption as a tool to supplement other measures that have resulted in a gradual increase in women's representation—the incremental track. They compare the cases of Costa Rica and Denmark to illustrate the differences between these two tracks. In the former, the introduction of a quota meant that women's representation increased from 19% to 35% in just one election. In the latter, a similar increase was only achieved over the course of 20 years and eight elections (Dahlerup and Freidenvall 2005).

In addition to the fast and incremental track narratives, I argue that there is a second axis of quota development, contrasting an 'endogenous' track with an 'exogenous' track. The existing literature on gender quotas tends to treat quota adoption as an 'exogenous shock' to a political system (Baldez 2006: 104; see also Bhavnani 2009: 24; Júlio and Tavares 2010). Kudva and Misra (2008) argue that literature tends to assume the impetus for quota adoption is an exogenous factor originating from outside local women's spaces and the domestic political sphere. They argue that in many cases of quota adoption, quotas can be considered endogenous developments, with quota reform being implemented from within the political system in which it will be implemented (Kudva and Misra 2008).

This does not preclude the existence of an exogenous model of quota adoption. Expanding on Kuda and Misra's argument, it can be argued that quotas that are to be implemented at the sub-national level but are passed at the national level should be considered exogenous developments, as the quota regulations are in effect being imposed on, rather than adopted by, the political institutions. Examples of this could include quotas for local government institutions that passed in the national legislature, or quotas passed by a colonial power that are imposed on territorial institutions. This latter model, exemplified by quota adoption in the French Pacific collectivities, is an example of this exogenous path.

The manner in which a quota is adopted—through endogenous or exogenous development—could theoretically influence the effectiveness of the quota. Variation in the impact of quotas between countries and parties is often attributed to the details of quota measures, and how well they relate to political institutions (see Krook 2009). Furthermore, suc-cessful quota adoption is often linked to the roles played by local actors, especially political elites, but also women's organisations, the judiciary and the general public (Krook 2009). In an exogenous track context, where the quota has been externally imposed and in some cases designed for a different political environment, and local actors are not necessarily directly involved in quota adoption, the effectiveness of quota measures could be diminished.

Assuming a binary distinction between endogenous and exogenous tracks of quota development, however, is problematic. As some scholars point out (Bush 2011; Krook 2009), domestic quota adoption can be greatly influenced by international actors, including inter-national organisations. The international diffusion of quotas, and the influence of transnational networks of activists, can therefore be exogenous aspects of quota development even in an endogenously driven case of quota adoption. Furthermore, quota adoption that is exogen-ously imposed on a political institution can still involve endogenous elements, for example the support of domestic political and civil society actors.

Nevertheless, a distinction between primarily endogenous quota adoption and primarily exogenous quota adoption can be made. I argue against the classification of all cases of quota adoption as 'exogenous shocks' to political institutions. There are both endogenous and exogenous models of quota development, and in most cases aspects of both will interact with each other in the process of quota adoption. I propose that the adoption of the parity laws in the French Pacific collectivities constitutes an example of primarily exogenous quota adoption.

The Parity Laws

France has been described as having 'a chronic history of women's under-representation in all aspects of its political system' (Murray 2009: 29). Women in France gained the right to vote and stand for elected office in 1944, and in the five decades that followed never accounted for more than 6% of seats in the legislative assembly (Bereni 2007). The first female prime minister, Edith Cresson, was appointed in 1991, although she held the post for less than a year. Prior to the implementation of the parity law in 1999, women made up less than 6% of the Senate and 11% of the Assembly, and held just 8% of mayoral posts (Berman 2005).

The argument for parity between women and men in legislatures was put forward by activists from the 1970s onward, although it first gained prominence in the late 1980s (Sénac-Slawinski 2008). The publication of the book *Au pouvoir citoyennes: liberté, egalité, parité*[2] by authors Françoise Gaspard, Claude Servan-Schreiber and Anne Le Gall (1992) was a turning point in the campaign for parity. Baudino (2003: 386) notes that parity had significant support from the general public, becoming a 'household word' as the campaign developed.

The campaign for parity culminated in two constitutional amendments that were passed on 18 July 1999. The first amendment states, 'the law favours the equal access of women and men to electoral mandates and elective functions', and the second, 'political parties and groups contribute to the implementation of this principle'. On 6 June 2000, enabling laws to implement the parity law provisions were passed. A new law was enacted in 2007 to strengthen parity provisions and enforce parity for municipal and regional executives (Bargel et al. 2010).

The effect of the parity laws in France varies across different political levels. Where parity was applied, the percentage of women elected to town councils more than doubled, from

21.4% to 47.5% (Lépinard 2006). This increase in female councillors did not translate to an equal increase in female mayors, with men still over-represented in mayoral posts to which parity regulation does not extend. The parity law has also improved women's representation at regional and European levels. At the national level, however, the parity law has been less effective, with Murray (2007: 569) calling the results of the 2002 legislative elections an 'unmitigated failure of parity'. Only 38.9% of candidates were women, and the results saw only a small increase in the number of female députés (Murray 2013). The 2007 legislative elections saw over 40% female candidates, and the number of female députés rose to 18.5%; in 2012, 40% of candidates and 27% of députés elected were women (Murray 2013). In senatorial elections, the laws first applied in 2001. In the 74 seats contested using a proportional representation (PR) voting system, the number of women elected quadrupled to 20, but in the 28 other seats contested the number of women elected remained static, at two (Southwell and Smith 2007).

Implementation of the Parity Laws in the French Pacific

The French overseas départements (departments) and collectivities are the areas of the world, outside of Europe, that are under French administrative control. This consists of three collectivities in the Pacific Islands region: Wallis and Futuna; French Polynesia; and New Caledonia. There are other French collectivities and départements in the Caribbean region, South America, and the Atlantic and Indian oceans.

Wallis and Futuna has the smallest population of the Pacific collectivities, with around 15,000 inhabitants. The colony of Wallis and Futuna was administrated by New Caledonia until it became a separate political entity in 1961. Wallis and Futuna has a Territorial Assembly of 20 seats. Politics in Wallis and Futuna has been historically a male-dominated sphere. Prior to the 1990s, no women had been elected to the Wallis and Futuna Territorial Assembly. For the first time in 1992, two women won seats (Drage 1995). In the following election, in 1998, two women were also elected, standing on lists of mostly female candidates (Bargel et al. 2010).

French Polynesia has a population of around 270,000. While the French Pacific territories had been removed from the United Nations List of Non-Self-Governing Territories in 1947, French Polynesia was re-inscribed in 2013.[3] Women in French Polynesia had some success in politics prior to the introduction of the parity law. The first female representative, Céline Oopa, was elected in 1961 (Bargel et al. 2010). Another woman, Huguette Hong Kiou, sat in the Assembly from 1984 to 1992 (Drage 1995). In the 1996 election, five women (12 per cent) won seats in the Assembly of French Polynesia (von Strokirch 2001).

New Caledonia is a Melanesian island group with a population of around 260,000. Unlike other overseas collectivities and departments of France, New Caledonia has a special status as defined in the French Constitution which allows it a greater degree of political autonomy (Maclellan 2005). As in French Polynesia, the 1956 Defferre Law led to the establishment of a Territorial Assembly, elected by New Caledonians through universal suffrage (Fisher 2013). From its establishment to 1999, there were no female members of the Territorial Assembly (Drage 1995).

In the second half of the twentieth century, New Caledonia was the site of a protracted struggle for independence from France, with the pro-independence movement reaching its height in the 1980s. A peace agreement was reached in 1988, giving New Caledonia greater rights of self-determination and guaranteeing a future referendum on independence. The Noumea Accord, signed in 1998, granted New Caledonia a separate political status to other territories in the French Constitution, created the provincial assemblies and 54-seat Congress, and delayed the referendum for a further 15–20 years (Fisher 2013). In the first post-Noumea Accord elections in 1999, in which the parity laws did not apply, nine women were elected (*Les Nouvelles Calédoniennes* 2004). In 2001, Déwé Gorodé, of the Palika Party,[4] was elected vice-president of New Caledonia. She was one of two female members of the 11-strong Cabinet. Prior to parity, around 10% of elected municipal positions were held by women (Berman 2005).

When the parity laws were adopted in France, it was assumed that they were to apply to all parts of France, including its overseas departments and collectivities (de Bonnefoy 2000a). On 8 March 2000, International Women's Day, the French Secretary of Overseas Territories, Jean-Jack Queyranne, confirmed that parity would apply in the overseas departments and collectivities as well as in the French mainland (*Les Nouvelles Calédoniennes* 2000c). While this line was held to by the French government, there was opposition to (as well as support for) the parity laws in the Pacific territories, as well as attempts in each territory to prevent or delay the implementation of all or some of the quota provisions.

The representative for Wallis and Futuna in the French Senate, Robert Laufoaulu, sought to amend the parity laws, to gain an exemption from the provisions that he felt would disadvantage Wallis and Futunan women (Bargel et al. 2010). In 2000, he put forward an amendment to exclude the territory from the provision mandating that equal numbers of men and women be present on party lists. He argued that the parity law would hinder rather than advance women's electoral chances in Wallis and Futuna, as women who had previously won election to the Territorial Assembly had stood on all-women lists, which would be prohibited under the new law. He requested an exemption for Wallis and Futuna so that the practice of all-women party lists could continue. The amendment was unsuccessful, and parity was duly applied in Wallis and Futuna from 2002 (Bargel et al. 2010).

In French Polynesia, politician Emile Vernaudon spearheaded a move to obtain an exemption for overseas territories from the provisions around strict alternation of male and female candidates on party lists (von Strokirch 2001). The amendment originally won support in the National Assembly, and later in the Senate with the backing of Gaston Flosse, the representative from French Polynesia. Ultimately, however, it was rejected by a law commission report, and the parity laws eventually passed without it (von Strokirch 2001).

In 2000, Simon Loueckhote, a member of the French Senate for New Caledonia, announced that he would seek to amend the parity laws to delay their implementation in the collectivity until the 2007 municipal elections (Claudel 2000a). Loueckhote, a member of the pro-independence party RPCR,[5] was a prominent figure in New Caledonian politics at that time, holding not only a senatorial seat but also the position of president of the New Caledonia Congress. The move was labelled a 'small bombshell' by the newspaper *Les Nouvelles Calédoniennes* (Claudel 2000a: 7). It was also criticised by Loueckhote's colleagues in the RPCR. Marie-Noëlle Thémereau, who at the time was the vice-president of the RPCR and would later serve as president of New Caledonia from 2004 to 2007, threatened to resign from the party if the amendment was tabled (de Bonnefoy 2000a). She labelled the proposed amendment 'a rear-guard, retrograde move' (quoted in de Bonnefoy 2000a: 8).

Opponents to the introduction of parity in New Caledonia used three main arguments (see Berman 2005). Firstly, they claimed women were not prepared to enter politics. Loueckhote argued that Kanak women in particular would not be prepared for politics, due to cultural reasons (Bargel et al. 2010). He claimed to have struggled to find women candidates to stand on his list in the preceding provincial elections, citing this experience as evidence of the need to delay the implementation of the parity laws (*Les Nouvelles Calédoniennes* 2000a).

The second argument used was that the parity laws would have a negative effect on Kanak culture and custom, as it was seen as constituting 'a fundamental change in its traditional concept of the role of women' (CDI 2002: 7). Members of the Customary Senate, an advisory body made up of Kanak elders, voiced fears that the parity laws would cause societal problems for the Kanak population (Berman 2005). Qenegei argued that the move would negatively affect Kanak society: 'this will disrupt the whole Melanesian environment' (quoted in Fléaux 2000: 4).

Finally, opponents of the parity laws argued that the law was a colonial imposition and a distraction from the fight for independence from France. When the Loueckhote amendment was put forward, an FLNKS spokesman criticised parity as a threat to the independence movement:

> The political arm of the FLNKS ... regrets that during this heated debate, certain politicians have hoped that the law on parity would apply 'ipso facto' in our country, thus calling into questions the will for decolonisation and self-government sanctioned by the Noumea Accord. (Quoted in Claudel 2000b: 2)

Kanak politician Nicole Waïa, however, questioned the idea that the parity laws threatened the decolonisation process: 'How does the fight for parity between men and women harm the process of decolonisation? For me, decolonisation should result in advancement, change, progress' (quoted in *Les Nouvelles Calédoniennes* 2000d: 8). The Loueckhote amendment was publicly condemned by New Caledonian women, who staged protests and sent a 1600-signature petition to the French Minister of the Interior in support of parity (de Bonnefoy 2000b; *Les Nouvelles Calédoniennes* 2000b).

Ultimately, none of the amendments to the parity laws proposed by French Pacific politicians were passed into law. Parity has been implemented in Wallis and Futuna in three territorial elections to date. The first election, in 2002, actually saw a drop in female legislators from the previous term, as only one woman was elected from a list in which she was in second place. Two more women gained seats in 2004 and 2005 when one male member resigned and another died, bringing the total number of female Assembly members to three (15%) for the term (Bargel et al. 2010). In the 2007 election, two women won seats. Both women had previously been elected to the Assembly in second position on party lists, but in 2007 were at the head of their own respective lists (Bargel et al. 2010). Shortly after the territorial election, one Assembly member was elected to serve in the French National Assembly, and he was replaced in his territorial seat by the next person on his list, a woman (Bargel et al. 2010). This again brought the women's representation level in the Territorial Assembly to 15%. In the 2012 election, four women were elected (20%).

French Polynesia, in contrast, saw a significant increase in women's representation in the Assembly following the 2001 election, the first under the parity laws. Twenty-two women won seats, and Lucette Taero was elected as the first woman president of the Assembly.[6] Six women were also appointed to the 17-seat Cabinet (von Strokirch 2002). This was a slight increase from the five women who held ministerial posts before 2001. In 2004, 27 women (47%) were elected to the Assembly, although the number of female ministers dropped to four (Bargel et al. 2010). After the 2013 election, there were 30 women (52%) members of the Assembly, although women only held two of eight ministerial positions.

When parity was first applied in New Caledonia in the provincial elections, in 2004, women's representation increased dramatically. In each of the three provincial assemblies, women made up 50% of the seats, and the Congress had 46.3% women's representation.

Furthermore, following the 2004 elections, Marie-Noëlle Thémereau was elected as the first female president of New Caledonia, while Gorodé was re-confirmed in her position as vice-president. Thémereau was founder and leader of the *Avenir Ensemble* party, which won 16 Congress seats in the 2004 election. Fraenkel cites the election of these two women to the head of government as evidence that 'women were well-prepared to take advantage of the new [parity] laws' (Fraenkel 2006: 84). Gorodé's party, Palika, also cited the appointments as examples of 'parity at the highest level' (Claudel 2001: 6). Berman (2005), however, notes that the Thémereau administration encountered a lot of resistance, especially from her former party, the *Rassemblement-UMP*.[7] Members of the *Rassemblement-UMP* resigned from the Cabinet hours after Thémereau and Gorodé were confirmed in their positions, thus bringing down the government.[8] Although Thémereau and Gorodé were eventually reinstated as president and vice-president, Berman (2005) argues:

> the resistance Mme. Thémereau encountered in forming a government substantiates the claim that women face difficulties in entering a male dominated political culture. The climate for women to become part of the political colonial establishment remains very chilly.

Thémereau resigned as president in 2007, and was replaced by Harold Martin. In the provincial election of 2009, women won 47.4% of the seats as in the three territorial assemblies, and 44.4% of seats in Congress. Maclellan (2009: 10) observes: 'New Caledonia's quota system has created an important mechanism for women to enter public life.'

It is important to note that parity at all political levels is yet to be achieved. Even after ten years of the parity law, women are still under-represented in political leadership positions at ministerial level and at mayoral level in the French Pacific. Given the low rates of women's political representation in the Pacific Islands region, however, the levels attained by the French Pacific territories are highly noteworthy. As New Caledonian politician Gaël Yanno has said: 'Without the law, this progress would never have been made' (Cochin 2009).

Quota Adoption in the French Pacific as an Exogenous Track Model

In the French Pacific, the parity laws were imposed from the external metropole and implemented in the territorial assemblies without requiring territorial-level legislation or even debate. The parity laws were developed in, and designed for, the political context of the French mainland, and thus their implementation in the Pacific collectivities could be viewed as essentially an inadvertent by-product of the larger quota campaign.

There are other cases of colonial quota adoption, where colonial powers have implemented quota policies in the political institutions of territories (Hughes et al. forthcoming). The first reserved seats for women system was introduced in India in the 1930s by the British government, a policy criticised by the pro-independence movement, and eventually abolished when independence was gained (Krook 2009). The British government introduced quotas in India through the Government of India Act in 1935. The Act dictated that six seats be reserved for women in the Council of State, and nine seats in the Federal Assembly.[9] They were indirectly elected by representatives sitting in the assemblies of the provinces. The gender quota, along with measures for other marginalised groups, were considered to be a tool to consolidate power: 'In India, reserved seats were initially viewed as a tool for preserving colonial domination by giving various groups a stake in maintaining the existing regime' (Krook 2009: 222).

The Indian government instituted reserved seats for women at the local governmental level in the 1980s; however, a gender quota has not been introduced at the national level despite campaigning from women's groups for a parliamentary quota. The British colony of India also encompassed what are now the independent states of Pakistan and Bangladesh. These states, therefore, have a shared colonial experience with gender quotas. In contrast to India, however, Pakistan introduced reserved seats for women after independence based on the colonial-era quota system (Rai et al. 2006), and currently has a gender quota requirement in its national legislature (Krook 2009). Bangladesh also has a reserved seats system in place (Rai 2005). While reserved seats are still in use in the former territories, they have strong colonial connotations. The term used to describe such systems in the area—'reservations'—is borrowed from the colonial-era legislation (Chowdhury 2003).

Colonial implementation of gender quotas, as seen in the case of the Government of India Act 1935, constitutes an exogenous track of quota adoption. Under this model, quotas are not adopted by the same political institution in which they will be implemented. Instead, quotas are imposed upon a political institution exogenously—in these colonial cases, by a metropolitan power. The adoption of the parity laws in the French Pacific collectivities reflects this exogenous track model, whereby parity was imposed externally from the political institutions of the French mainland.

The classification of the quota adoption in the French Pacific collectivities as an 'exogenous' track development would be challenged by a French republican universalist worldview, in which the French republic encompasses both mainland France and the overseas territories and is indivisible as a political construct. Even if one recognises the French Pacific territorial political institutions as separate political constructs from those in the French mainland, there are still arguably endogenous aspects to the quota adoption in the collectivities, including the active role of the New Caledonian women's movement in advocating for quotas, and the actions of representatives of the collectivities in the French Senate in attempting to block their introduction.

As noted previously, a key issue raised in opposition to the implementation of the parity laws in New Caledonia was that the quota was a colonial imposition. The response from quota advocates was that it was no different to any other law passed by the metropole and imposed in the territory: 'All laws here are colonial laws' (Joredie, quoted in Berman 2005). Implementation of the parity laws in the other parts of the French Pacific occurred in similar political environments. Shineberg (1988: 93) writes of French Polynesia: 'all the Territorial institutions are creatures of the French parliament and may be changed according to the latter's will.' In the case of the French Pacific collectivities, exogenous track quota adoption can thus be situated in a context in which the imposition of laws from the external metropole is an acknowledged facet of territorial politics.

A significant factor to consider when regarding cases of 'exogenous' track quota adoption in colonial contexts is the impact of quota design. In the case of the French Pacific collectivities, a gender quota that was designed for the French political system was applied to territorial institutions. In the collectivities, the list PR electoral system used meant that parties had to comply with the quota requirements or be ruled ineligible to contest the election; in the elections for the French National Assembly, parties who do not have equal numbers of male and female candidates have to pay a financial penalty, but are still permitted to contest the election. In practice, this means that the parity laws have had a transformative effect on gender balance in territorial politics in French Polynesia and New Caledonia that far exceeds their effect in the French National Assembly.

Conclusion

Dahlerup and Freidenvall (2005) identify two distinct models of quota adoption, the fast track and the incremental track. In this article, I have proposed a further axis focusing on exogenous versus endogenous tracks. The distinction between these two tracks lies in the process of quota adoption—whether it is carried out within the political institution in which the quota will be implemented (the 'endogenous' track), or external to the institution (the 'exogenous' track). The process of implementing the parity laws in the French Pacific can be classified as primarily exogenous track quota adoption.

It should be noted that there were endogenous elements in the quota adoption process, exemplified by debate over the parity laws in the French Pacific, most notably in New Caledonia, and legislative attempts to block or delay quota adoption in each of the territories, as recounted above. The classification of quota adoption in the collectivities as exogenous would also be challenged by a French republican universalist perspective, in which France—the French mainland and its overseas territories—is a unified political construct and thus unable to be divided into separate political entities. Nevertheless, as implementation in the collectivities was largely a by-product of the metropolitan quota campaign and legislative process, it can constitute an example of primarily exogenous quota adoption.

While quota implementation in the French Pacific was arguably a mere side effect of the larger campaign for gender parity in France, its impact on the proportion of women elected in the collectivities has been significant. Women's representation in the legislatures of New Caledonia and French Polynesia has increased dramatically, to over 40% women's representation in the New Caledonian Congress, and over 50% in the French Polynesian Assembly. The effect of the parity laws in Wallis and Futuna has been less pronounced, largely due to a comparatively weaker party system. Despite the uneven impact of the parity laws across both the French mainland and the collectivities, the significant gains in women's representation made particularly in New Caledonia and French Polynesia highlight the potential for effective quota implementation in an exogenous track process.

ACKNOWLEDGEMENTS

An earlier version of this article was presented at the European Conference on Politics and Gender, Universitat Pompeu Fabra, Barcelona, 21–23 March 2013.

NOTES

1. Excluding the French Pacific collectivities; adapted from IPU (2014).
2. 'To power (female) citizens : liberty, equality, parity'.
3. New Caledonia had previously been re-inscribed in 1986 (Fisher 2013). Of the three French Pacific collectivities, only Wallis and Futuna is currently not listed on the UN List of Non-Self-Governing Territories.
4. *Parti de Libération Kanak* (Party of Kanak Liberation).
5. *Rassemblement pour une Calédonie dans la République*. The party was affiliated with the French political party *Rassemblement pour une République* (RPR). In 2002, the party changed its name to *Rassemblement-UMP*, after the RPR merged with other centre-right French parties to form the *Union pour un Mouvement Populaire* (UMP).

6. The President of the Assembly serves a similar function as a parliamentary Speaker.
7. Formerly the *Rassemblement pour une Calédonie dans la République* (RPCR).
8. Under the power-sharing provisions of the 1998 Noumea Accord, all parties that win a certain percentage of the seats in Congress are entitled to seats in Cabinet, proportionate to their share of the vote. The members of Cabinet then elect a president and vice-president. If one party in Cabinet resigns, the government is dissolved and a new Cabinet must be elected by Congress.
9. The Council of State was the upper legislative house, and the Federal Assembly the lower legislative house, of the British colony of India, as established by the Government of India Act 1935. The reserved seats for women made up a small fraction of the legislative assembly seats, below 4% in both the lower and upper houses (Krook 2009: 59).

REFERENCES

BALDEZ, LISA. 2006. The pros and cons of gender quota laws: what happens when you kick men out and let women in? *Politics and Gender* 2 (1): 102–9.

BARGEL, LUCIE, STÉPHANIE GUYON and ISABELLE S. RETTIG. 2010. *Assessment of the Application of the 'Parity Law' in New Caledonia, French Polynesia and Wallis and Futuna (April–June 2007)*. Noumea: Secretariat of the Pacific Community.

BAUDINO, CLAUDIE. 2003. Parity reform in France: promises and pitfalls. *Review of Policy Research* 20 (3): 385–400.

BERENI, LAURE. 2007. French feminists renegotiate republican universalism: the gender parity campaign. *French Politics* 5 (3): 191–209.

BERMAN, ALAN. 2005. The law on gender parity in politics in France and New Caledonia: a window into the future or more of the same? *Oxford University Comparative Law Forum 2*, available at ouclf. iuscomp.org, accessed 14 August 2014.

BHAVNANI, RIKHIL R. 2009. Do electoral quotas work after they are withdrawn? Evidence from a natural experiment in India. *American Political Science Review* 103 (1): 23–35.

DE BONNEFOY, SANDRINE. 2000a. Simon Loueckhote renonce à son amendement sur la parité. *Les Nouvelles Calédoniennes*, 24 February, p. 8.

DE BONNEFOY, SANDRINE. 2000b. La croisade des Femmes en colère. *Les Nouvelles Calédoniennes*, 24 March, p. 8.

BUSH, SARAH S. 2011. International politics and the spread of quotas for women in legislatures. *International Organization* 65 (1): 103–37.

CENTRE FOR DEMOCRATIC INSTITUTIONS (CDI). 2002. *Report of the Third Pacific Parliamentary Retreat, Brisbane, 3–7 December 2011*. Canberra: CDI.

CHOWDHURY, NAJIMA. 2003. Bangladesh's experience – dependence and marginality in politics. In *The Implementation of Quotas: Asian Experiences*, Quota Workshops Report Series, Stockholm: International Institute for Democracy and Electoral Assistance (IDEA).

CLAUDEL, BRIGITTE. 2000a. Simon Loueckhote : ' *Cet amendement est celui de bon sens*' . *Les Nouvelles Calédoniennes*, 3 March, p. 7.

CLAUDEL, BRIGITTE. 2000b. Le revirement du FLNKS. *Les Nouvelles Calédoniennes*, 9 March, p. 2.

CLAUDEL, BRIGITTE. 2001. Déwé Gorodey vice-présidente du gouvernement Frogier. *Les Nouvelles Calédoniennes*, 6 April, p. 6.

COCHIN, CORALIE. 2009. La parité homme-femme ne fait plus débat. *Les Nouvelles Calédoniennes*, 8 April.

DAHLERUP, DRUDE and LENITA FREIDENVALL. 2005. Quotas as a 'fast track' to equal representation for women: why Scandinavia is no longer the model. *International Feminist Journal of Politics* 7 (1): 26–48.

DRAGE, JEAN. 1995. The exception, not the rule: a comparative analysis of women's political activity in Pacific Islands countries. *Pacific Studies* 18 (4): 61–93.

FISHER, DENISE. 2013. *France in the South Pacific*. Canberra: ANU Press.

FLÉAUX, DIDIER. 2000. La sagesse de César Qenegei. *Les Nouvelles Calédoniennes*, 26–27 February, p. 4.

FRAENKEL, JON. 2006. The impact of electoral systems on women's representation in Pacific parliaments. In *A Woman's Place is in the House – The House of Parliament; Research to Advance Women's Political Representation in Forum Island Countries*. Suva: Pacific Islands Forum Secretariat, pp. 57–106.

GASPARD, FRANÇOISE, CLAUDE SERVAN-SCHREIBER and ANNE LE GALL. 1992. *Au Pouvoir, Citoyennes! Liberté, Egalité, Parité*. Paris: Seuil.

HUGHES, MELANIE M., MONA LENA KROOK and PAMELA PAXTON. Forthcoming. Transnational women's activism and the global diffusion of gender quotas. *International Studies Quarterly*.

INTER-PARLIAMENTARY UNION (IPU). 2014. Women in National Parliaments. 1 April. Available at http://www.ipu.org/wmn-e/classif.htm, accessed 16 May 2014.

JÚLIO, PAULO and JOSÉ TAVARES. 2010. The good, the bad, and the different: can gender quotas raise the quality of politicians? *CEPR Discussion Paper No. 7917*.

KROOK, MONA LENA. 2009. *Quotas for Women in Politics: Gender and Candidate Selection Reform Worldwide*. New York: Oxford University Press.

KUDVA, NEEMA and KAJRI MISRA. 2008. Gender quotas, the politics of presence, and the feminist project: what does the Indian experience tell us? *Signs* 34 (1): 49–73.

LÉPINARD, ELÉONORE. 2006. Identity without politics: framing the parity laws and their implementation in French local politics. *Social Politics* 13 (1): 30–58.

LES NOUVELLES CALÉDONIENNES. 2000a. Parité sur les listes électorales : les femmes citoyennes indignées, 4–5 March, p. 6.

LES NOUVELLES CALÉDONIENNES. 2000b. Cinq cents signatures contre l'amendement Loueckhote, 9 March, p. 7.

LES NOUVELLES CALÉDONIENNES. 2000c. Jean-Jack Queyranne : ' La parité s'impose Outre-Mer comme en Métropole' , 10 March, p. 10.

LES NOUVELLES CALÉDONIENNES. 2000d. Nicole Waïa demande un débat au Congrès sur la parité hommes femmes en politique, 25–26 March, p. 8.

LES NOUVELLES CALÉDONIENNES. 2004. Le vrai changement viendra-t-il des femmes?, 7 May.

MACLELLAN, NIC. 2005. From Eloi to Europe: interactions with the ballot box in New Caledonia. *Commonwealth and Comparative Politics* 43 (3): 394–418.

MACLELLAN, NIC. 2009. New government in New Caledonia: the May 2009 elections in a French Pacific territory. *State Society and Governance in Melanesia Briefing Note 3/2009*.

MURRAY, RAINBOW. 2007. How parties evaluate compulsory quotas: a study of the implementation of the 'parity' law in France. *Parliamentary Affairs* 60 (4): 568–84.

MURRAY, RAINBOW. 2008. Fifty years of feminising France's fifth republic. *Modern and Contemporary France* 16 (4): 469–82.

MURRAY, RAINBOW. 2009. Was 2007 a landmark or a let-down for women's political representation in France? *Representation* 45 (1): 29–38.

MURRAY, RAINBOW. 2013. Towards parity democracy? Gender in the 2012 French legislative elections. *Parliamentary Affairs* 66 (1): 197–212.

RAI, SHIRIN M. 2005. Reserved seats in South Asia: a regional perspective. In *Women in Parliament: Beyond Numbers*, edited by Julie Ballington and Azza Karam. Stockholm: International Institute for Democracy and Electoral Assistance (IDEA), pp. 174–84.

RAI, SHIRIN M., FARZANA BARI, NAZMUNESSA MAHTAB and BIDYUT MOHANTY. 2006. South Asia: gender quotas and the politics of empowerment – a comparative study. In *Women, Quotas and Politics*, edited by Drude Dahlerup. New York: Routledge, pp. 222–45.

SECRETARIAT OF THE PACIFIC COMMUNITY (SPC). 2007. Political parity law 'a success' in Pacific. 1 June. Available at http://www.scoop.co.nz/stories/WO0706/S00018.htm, accessed 16 May 2014.

SÉNAC-SLAWINSKI, REJANE. 2008. Justifying parity in France after the passage of the so-called parity laws and the electoral application of them: the ideological tinkering of political party officials (UMP and PS) and women's NGOs. *French Politics* 6 (3): 234–56.

SHINEBERG, BARRY. 1988. The image of France. In *French Polynesia*, edited by Nancy J. Pollock and Ron Crocombe. Suva: University of the South Pacific, pp. 78–98.

SOUTHWELL, PRISCILLA L. and COURTNEY P. SMITH. 2007. Equality of recruitment: gender parity in French National Assembly elections. *The Social Science Journal* 44 (1): 83–90.

VON STROKIRCH, KARIN. 2001. French Polynesia. *The Contemporary Pacific* 13 (1): 225–35.

VON STROKIRCH, KARIN. 2002. French Polynesia. *The Contemporary Pacific* 14 (1): 213–19.

WHY ARE REPRESENTATIONAL GUARANTEES ADOPTED FOR WOMEN AND MINORITIES? COMPARING CONSTITUENCY FORMATION AND ELECTORAL QUOTA DESIGN WITHIN COUNTRIES

Elin Bjarnegård and Pär Zetterberg

This article explores the underlying motives for ensuring the political inclusion of marginalised groups. More specifically, it analyses whether laws guaranteeing representation are designed differently for women and minorities and, if so, whether these differences correspond to normative arguments for group representation. We use a novel research strategy by comparing quota designs in all countries that have adopted quotas for both groups. Theoretically, we reconceptualise the relevant distinction between quota types by focusing on whether a special constituency is created or not. We identify substantial differences in quota design between the two groups. Minorities tend to be guaranteed representation through the creation of special constituencies, whereas gender quotas more commonly imply integration into pre-existing constituencies. The analysis largely supports those who argue that quotas for minorities aim to increase the autonomy of the group in question while gender quotas are adopted with the intention to integrate women into the political system.

A recent trend in processes of constitution-making and electoral reform is the provision of guarantees of political representation for marginalised groups. Granting women and minorities increased access to representation is common, for instance, in democratisation processes and in post-conflict societies and peace agreements. Today, the constitutions or election laws of more than 30 countries include electoral quotas[1] for the wide variety of different groups (e.g., ethnic, religious, occupational and age-based) that commonly go under the name of 'minority groups' (e.g., Krook and O'Brien 2010; Reynolds 2005). State-mandated gender quotas have been adopted in approximately 50 countries across the globe (Dahlerup 2007; Krook 2009). Yet, a fairly limited number of studies analyse and compare the adoption of quota policies for both groups (notable exceptions include Htun 2004; Htun and Ossa 2013; Hughes 2011; Krook and O'Brien 2010); most research on electoral quota adoption concerns either quotas for women (e.g., Dahlerup 2006; Krook 2009; Meier 2004; Murray et al. 2012) or quotas for minorities (e.g., Bird 2014; Lublin and Wright 2013; Pande 2003; Reynolds 2005, 2011). We thus know relatively little about the potentially different underlying motives for ensuring the political inclusion of different groups.

This article aims at filling this gap by analysing whether laws guaranteeing representation are designed differently for women and minorities and, if so, whether these variations correspond to distinct normative arguments for group representation. Literature on group representation suggests that the roots of political exclusion differ across groups and that representational guarantees may therefore seek to remedy distinct problems. Whereas the introduction of quota policies for minorities may rest on an underlying motive to separate the group in question from the ordinary electoral procedures, some argue, the adoption of gender quotas may be driven by the aim to better integrate women into the existing system (Kymlicka 1995). We analyse these propositions by using a novel research strategy, as well as a new and innovative conceptual distinction between quota types. Theoretically, we move beyond the conventional distinction between reserved seats and quotas for candidates (e.g., Dahlerup 2006; Franceschet et al. 2012; Htun 2004; Krook 2009) to explore whether special (separate or overlapping) constituencies are created for the targeted group, or whether the quota is instead incorporated into existing constituencies. We suggest that such a distinction better captures the extent to which an electoral quota is designed to separate or integrate the targeted group (see also Krook 2014).

Empirically, we compare the design of electoral quotas for women and minorities in a specific set of countries: those that have adopted quotas for both groups. A within-country comparison enables us to hold constant particular historical and country-specific factors that some scholars on quota adoption have suggested account for cross-group differences in quota design (Krook and O'Brien 2010). If normative arguments about separation and integration do correspond to lawmakers' separate justifications for why representational guarantees are warranted, quota legislation for minorities will more commonly stipulate constituency formation whereas gender quota policies will more often be designed to operate within the pre-existing constituency boundaries.

By conducting a detailed analysis of constitutions and election laws in 13 countries (or territories) we identify a clear correspondence between normative arguments for group representation and actual policy designs. Whereas gender quotas are implemented within the existing electoral structures, representational guarantees for minority groups in most of cases entail the formation of a special constituency defining who may stand for election and who is allowed to vote. The analysis thus contributes conceptually, methodologically and empirically to building a comparative research agenda on electoral quotas, and more broadly to increased understanding of the underlying motives for including different groups in policy-making.

Groups and Representation: Problems and Solutions

Although normative theorists often compare arguments for the representation of different groups (e.g., Kymlicka 1995; Mansbridge 1999; Young 2000), there have been relatively few systematic empirical comparisons of how quotas are designed for women and minority groups (but see Htun 2004; Krook and O'Brien 2010). As of yet, we do not know the extent to which quotas for different groups function in the same way and thus can be studied in the same manner.

Htun (2004) argues that ethnicity is different from gender as a political cleavage. Whereas gender cuts across ideological and partisan differences, she claims that ethnicity does, to a larger extent, coincide with such differences. Consequently, she suggests that 'different remedies for under-representation are logically appropriate for each group' (2004: 439).

Htun argues that ethnic minorities are suited to self-reinforcing measures that provide the group in question with certain autonomy. For women, on the other hand, self-cancelling remedies integrating the targeted group into the regular political process are more appropriate. Analysing electoral democracies, she points out that different types of quotas are adopted for women versus minority groups (Htun 2004).

We take these claims as our starting point. In order to fully understand to what extent policy designs differ according to perceptions of the groups in question, however, we argue for moving beyond a focus on group characteristics to take the actors behind the quota design—the lawmakers—into account. To do so, we make use of Bacchi's (1999) 'What's the Problem?' approach, which challenges the conventional view of public policy as a simple government response to an exogenous problem. Governments, Bacchi claims, do not just react to problems; they are active creators of problems. How problems are perceived shapes how they are discussed and which solutions are deemed appropriate. 'At its most basic, the insight is commonsensical – how we perceive or think about something will affect what we think ought to be done about it' (1999: 1). Critically analysing the policy regulations themselves, we illuminate problem descriptions that form the basis for specific electoral quota designs.

The Problems: Normative Arguments for Group Representation

There is a long-standing scholarly discussion about the origins of and remedies for the political exclusion of marginalised groups in normative work (e.g., Kymlicka 1995; Mansbridge 1999; Phillips 2005; Williams 1998; Young 2000). The debate concerns the legitimacy of different arguments for group representation. The discussion has centered on when, why and for whom special measures should be considered, as well as on appropriate measures for different groups. It is argued that certain groups, under certain circumstances, experience problems that justify representational guarantees. These normative arguments thus rest on specific problem descriptions that are based on interpretations of the origin of exclusion. Fraser (1995) discusses two different types of goals for groups when they seek remedy for injustices: socioeconomic redistribution or recognition of cultural difference. These two demands neatly correspond to the two common and legitimate grounds for guaranteeing group representation identified by Kymlicka (1995): systemic discrimination and self-government.

The systemic discrimination argument applies to groups in society that have historically been oppressed and therefore are also disadvantaged in the political process (cf. Young 1989, 1990). As Kymlicka (1995: 141) argues, 'the historical domination of some groups by other groups has left a trail of barriers and prejudices that makes it difficult for historically disadvantaged groups to participate effectively in the political process'. Importantly, from this point of view, any guarantees should aim for a society in which discrimination no longer takes place and where active measures for group representation are no longer needed. In other words, any remedies should be of a temporary character, only to be in place until the group is fully integrated into the polity. Giving this group special representation is both a compensation for past discrimination and an attempt to work against future discrimination by redistributing power.

The self-government argument, on the other hand, usually applies to groups in society like national minorities, whose different cultural identities and specificities have not been sufficiently recognised. For these groups, a certain degree of political autonomy is needed 'to ensure full and free development of their cultures and the best interests of their people'

(Kymlicka 1995: 27). Self-government is, thus, an argument about autonomy by separation from the regular system, a bid to make the group permanently politically relevant.[2]

Translating this discussion, we suggest systemic discrimination describes why women have been excluded from politics. Women have simply not stood the same chances of being nominated and elected as their male counterparts; the 'problem' is thus that women have not been sufficiently integrated into the political system. Minority groups, on the other hand, have suffered from lack of sufficient autonomy and self-determination; the 'problem' is therefore that minorities risk being consumed by the political system because they are not sufficiently separated from it. Thus, problem diagnoses for women and for minorities appear to be somewhat different.

The Solutions: Designing Electoral Quotas

Moving from problem descriptions to solutions, it is important to note that different solutions are indeed possible. Measures to ensure the increased representation of marginalised groups can range from an extension of practices already taking place in electoral institutions, such as drawing the boundaries of constituencies so that they correspond to 'communities of interest', to more direct interventions like quotas for legislatures. Even among electoral quotas there is considerable variation in design. We now take a closer look at empirical research on quota designs for different groups. The two main comparative, cross-national studies on the subject do not reach the same conclusions.

In an empirical analysis of electoral democracies, Htun (2004) claims that women tend to gain candidate quotas, whereas minorities more commonly receive reserved seats. Candidate quotas require political parties to put a certain number of people from the targeted group on candidate lists. Reserved seats, on the other hand, refer to a minimum number of parliamentary seats earmarked for individuals of an under-represented group. In line with Htun's argument that gender is a cross-cutting cleavage, candidate quotas are suitable for women because they target parties' internal nomination processes. Reserved seats, on the other hand, are often, but not always, add-on seats, filled after the election (Krook 2009). According to Htun, reserved seats suit minority groups because these grant them a degree of autonomy and independence from the system, cementing group difference.

Krook and O'Brien (2010), however, argue that the match between targeted groups and quota designs is far from perfect. In a global analysis, they demonstrate that women receive both candidate quotas and reserved seats: almost 40% of gender quotas entail reservation. Minority representation, on the other hand, is almost always ensured by reserved seats. Krook and O'Brien suggest that contextual factors, rather than group characteristics, explain why governments choose one design over another. According to them, historical differences and transnational influences explain why particular types of quotas are common in certain regions. Reserved seats are more common—for women and ethnic groups alike—in Africa, Asia and the Middle East, whereas candidate quotas are more common in Latin America (mainly legislative quotas) and Europe (mainly party quotas) where, on the other hand, quotas for minority groups are less common. A study by Matland (2006) makes a similar observation, suggesting that countries with reserved seats for ethnic minorities tend to expand their use to women (Matland 2006).

We are thus left with two different accounts. On the one hand, Htun (2004) suggests that there are systematic differences in quota design for the two groups, implying that lawmakers have distinct motives for ensuring the political inclusion of women and minorities. On the other hand, Krook and O'Brien's (2010) study observes that women often receive the same quota as minorities. This would imply that contextual factors, rather than group characteristics, influence choices of quota design. We attempt to settle this issue by taking country-specific factors into account with a research strategy that helps unveil potential differences in the motives behind quota adoption.

Research Strategy: Same Country, Different Quota Designs?

Our research strategy qualifies previous research in two ways. First, we take contextual factors into account (cf. Krook and O'Brien 2010) by selecting only those cases in which quotas have been adopted for *both* women and minorities. Strategic case selection eliminates country-specific or regional contextual factors as an explanation for any cross-group differences in quota design. Second, we propose an improved distinction between quota types. We argue that the relevant question is not necessarily whether quotas target the nomination stage (candidate quotas) or the election stage (reserved seats) of the recruitment process (cf. Htun 2004). There are also relevant differences within quota types. Certain reserved seats designs, for instance, are more integrated into the ordinary political process than others— for example, some give voters the chance to directly elect representatives to reserved seats, while others give the power of appointment to the president or the prime minister (see also Dahlerup 2006; Krook 2009; Matland 2006). We suggest that a crucial question is whether policy-makers, when designing quotas, create new constituencies for targeted groups or establish guarantees within already existing constituencies. Constituencies put limits on who is allowed to vote and stand for election; in this way, they define the relationship between voters and representatives by circumscribing *competition* and the *electorate* (cf. Kymlicka 1995).

If policy-makers intend to separate certain groups from the ordinary electoral order to ensure that they are permanently politically relevant, an efficient way would be to create new special constituencies for these groups. We thus explore whether there are differences with respect to constituency formation between women and minorities. We anticipate that quota policies more commonly imply the creation of new, separate or overlapping, electoral districts for minorities than for women. The rationale is that constituency formation represents a solution to minority groups' lack of autonomy and self-determination, granting them some degree of independence in order to safeguard their group specificity. For women, on the other hand, quotas seek to increase women's opportunities to be treated in the same manner as their male counterparts, thus integrating women within already established constituency boundaries, with the goal being to eliminate the effects of past discrimination and render gender an unimportant political factor.

Analysing the content of legislative texts, we assess, first, whether quota policies assign new constituencies to targeted groups. Such an analysis enables us to assess whether there is a difference in the guarantees assigned to women and minorities. It also provides us with the opportunity to determine whether potential differences correspond to normative theories about group representation. Our assumption is that the way in which quota policies are formulated in constitutions and election laws can be interpreted as a manifestation of the underlying motives and intentions of lawmakers.

Second, our framework permits us to examine potential differences in the degree of separation. Whereas quotas implemented within existing constituencies do not limit competition and the electorate for the group in question, the formation of new constituencies can do so to varying degrees. Thus, where both women and minorities are assigned special constituencies, we examine how legislation is designed and worded with respect to who is entitled to run for the 'extra constituency seats' and who elects these representatives. Our expectation is that, even when new constituencies are created for both groups, the competition and electorate will be more limited in quotas for minorities versus women.

In all, we study regulations in 13 countries (or territories) that have adopted measures for both women and minorities in the single or lower house of parliament: Afghanistan, Burundi,[3] China, France, Jordan, Niger, Pakistan, Palestine, Portugal, Rwanda, Taiwan, Tanzania and Uganda.[4] We used two main sources: the Inter-Parliamentary Union's PARLINE database (IPU 2013) and the International Foundation for Electoral System's Election Guide (IFES 2013). Both databases contain information about election laws and constitutions. When they lacked the detail our analysis requires, we consulted the original constitution or election law.[5]

Results

Our results indicate that lawmakers, within a single country, are likely to design quotas differently for women and minorities. In a majority of the cases, new electoral districts are designed for minorities but not for women, and in no case do policy-makers assign women special constituencies and integrate minorities within the existing electoral districts. In those cases where new constituencies are created for both groups, the design of the constituencies is generally geared towards more separation for minorities. In three cases, however, there are no differences between women and minorities in terms of degree of separation.

Constituency Formation for Minorities but not for Women

In most of the cases (8 of 13), we can see a difference in quota design for women and certain, primarily smaller, minorities in terms of whether they are assigned new special constituencies. In this group, including Afghanistan, Burundi (in the case of Twa), China, France, Jordan, Niger, Portugal and Taiwan, policy-makers have chosen to provide minorities with new, separate or overlapping, constituencies whereas quotas for women are more firmly integrated into the existing political process.

Within this group, France, Niger, Portugal and Taiwan show clear similarities. Gender quotas are designed so as to require parties to put more women on their proportional (PR) lists. Women elected through quotas are thus not even discernible from other candidates; they compete on the same terms as all other candidates and for votes from the same set of voters. Quotas for minorities, on the other hand, are designed so as to create new, separate or overlapping, constituencies for minority groups. Only voters registered in that district can vote for the group in question, and minority candidates only compete with other minority candidates.

Starting with Niger, eight seats in the National Assembly are reserved for the Tuareg. Being a nomadic population, the Tuareg do not occupy a particular territory. While the 10% gender quota is integrated into the ordinary PR lists for the eight constituencies corresponding to regions, the quota for the Tuaregs specifies a creation of a different set of eight constituencies, where a first-past-the-post (FPTP) system is used. Only Tuareg vote in those territorially overlapping constituencies, and Tuareg compete against Tuareg candidates only. Additionally, the Tuareg population votes for the Tuareg seats only.

Taiwan follows a similar logic. In a mixed election system, 79 seats are elected from constituencies, while 34 seats are proportionally distributed. Among the 79 constituency-based seats, 73 seats emanate from FPTP single-member constituencies. The remaining six representatives are elected from two specially created, territorially overlapping, three-member constituencies, in which only the indigenous Austronesian inhabitants of Taiwan can vote and stand for election. The gender quota, on the other hand, operates in the parallel PR system. Among party-list candidates, 50% have to be women. This implies that women compete against men, and that both men and women vote for the female candidates.

In addition to gender quotas, France and Portugal both guarantee representation to expatriate communities. Just as in Niger and Taiwan, quotas for women apply to the candidate lists in each country's PR system. In contrast, expatriate communities are guaranteed representation through the creation of a territorially separate worldwide constituency, to which French or Portuguese citizens who live abroad are ascribed. Just as in any other constituency, only voters registered in that particular electoral district can vote, and candidates only compete with candidates from the same district.[6]

Afghanistan and Jordan serve as good illustrations of the usefulness of re-conceptualising the distinction between quota types. Although seats are reserved for both women and minorities, guarantees for minorities are more geared towards separation than those for women. Afghanistan's constitution from 2004 stipulates that 68 of 249 seats (27%) should be reserved for women. If women do not win their seats outright, the women who received the most votes, without being elected, are appointed until all 68 seats are filled. Another ten seats are reserved for a nomadic population, the Kuchis. The new nationwide Kuchi constituency overlaps with the other electoral districts. All Kuchis are granted special *Kuchi-cards* and can vote in designated Kuchi polling stations, only for the Kuchi seats.

There is thus a discernible difference between the reserved seats for women and for the Kuchi minority. The distribution of the reserved seats for women is based on the ordinary election, such that the women who fill these seats have competed with other candidates, male and female, for the same voters. No separate constituencies are created. The 'best-loser' system can indeed be interpreted as a way of integrating women into the electoral game, while giving them a 'boost' to compensate for disadvantages they might have in elections, in the long run levelling out the electoral playing field so that women can compete on the same terms as men. On the other hand, Kuchis do not compete at all with non-Kuchi candidates, nor are they accountable to a non-Kuchi constituency.

Similarly, the 2010 Election Law of Jordan stipulates that 10% of the 120 seats should be reserved for women. In addition, the law specifies that nine seats should be reserved for Christians and three seats for Circassians or Chechens. Within the 96 remaining seats, distributed among Muslim candidates,[7] nine are reserved for Bedouins. The quota for women is allocated among the Muslim seats, according to a best-loser logic. Unlike the Afghani design, however, these 12 seats are reserved for women, regardless of how many 'ordinary' seats women win. The rest of the seats are distributed through specific constituencies in which only members of the specific group (Chechens/Circassians, Bedouins and Muslims) have the right to vote, similar to the Afghani pattern.

Burundi is a special case because of distinct quotas for different ethnic groups. Burundi ends up in this classification when comparing the quota for women with the quota for the Twa ethnic group.[8] Just as in Niger, Taiwan, France and Portugal, there is a gender quota for candidate lists (30%). Thus, female politicians operate within the same constituency as their male counterparts. The Twa minority group, on the other hand, is guaranteed representation through reserved seats. However, the three Twa representatives are not directly elected to the reserved seats. The Election Commission formally appoints the parliamentarians from the Twa minority. Although the Twa representatives are not directly elected by voters, we suggest that a specific 'constituency' has been created. The representatives all come from Twa-specific organisations which nominate the candidates to the Election Commission.

China is different, in the sense that none of the almost 3,000 delegates to the National People's Congress (NPC) are elected through universal suffrage. Instead, they are elected within the organisational structure of the Communist Party, by the Local People's Congresses (LPCs) from around the country. Although it is difficult to discuss the relationship between representatives and their electorates in contexts where representatives are appointed rather than elected, with the limited data at our disposal we do discern a difference between the groups with respect to constituencies. The Electoral Law of the NPC and the LPCs rather vaguely stipulates that 'there shall be an appropriate number of women deputies, and the proportion thereof shall be raised gradually'. It is up to the LPCs to ensure that there is an 'appropriate' number of women on the lists. However, in contrast to the case of women, the LPCs are not the only bodies to elect members of specific ethnic groups to the NPC: the Communist Party has adopted a system in which the Standing Committee of the NPC reserves the right to appoint an additional 26 minority delegates. Thus, some of the minority delegates are accountable to a constituency other than all the other delegates, namely the national party elite of the Standing Committee of the NPC. By thus forming an extra overlapping constituency of sorts, the minority quota is less integrative than the gender quota.

Constituency Formation for Women and Minorities, Different Limitations on Electorate

Assessing differences in quota design through the lens of constituency formation thus helps us to unveil the logic behind quota adoption for different groups in eight of the cases. However, in six remaining cases this first step is unable to provide us with a comprehensive understanding. In Uganda, Rwanda and Tanzania, new constituencies have been created for *both* women and minorities. Importantly, just as in Burundi (in the case of the Twa) and China, these constituencies do not necessarily consist of electoral districts in which representatives are directly elected by voters within the area. Rather, a specific institution or organisation has been given the right to appoint representatives.

As both women and minorities are assigned special constituencies in these three countries, we look closer at the main features of the constituencies, with respect to who is entitled to compete for these 'extra constituency seats' and who elects, or appoints, the representatives. We find that there is no open electoral competition with non-members of the group. However, we find a difference across these countries with respect to group accountability.

Starting with Uganda, in addition to the 35% reserved seats for women, the 1995 Constitution also distributes special seats to workers, youth, the disabled and the army. Quotas for women and minorities are similar in the sense that a new set of constituencies have been created so that competition for the seats takes place only within the group. However, the ways in which representatives are elected to these seats differ. Representatives for workers, youth, the disabled and the army are indirectly elected by electoral colleges populated by local leaders of these groups. The reserved seats for women, on the other hand, are designed differently. From 2006 onwards, women are no longer elected by electoral colleges but via direct election. A new set of larger and territorially overlapping electoral districts have been created. Both men and women vote for who will enter the National Assembly in the 'women's seats'. Therefore, quotas for women in Uganda are more geared towards integration than are minority quotas.

In Rwanda, quotas for women and two minority groups—young people and disabled persons—were adopted in the constitutional reform process that followed the civil war. In both these cases, reserved seats are filled through special arrangements outside of the established constituency boundaries. Similar to Uganda, the quota design stipulates that young people as well as disabled persons are elected via functional decentralisation through the national organisation of each of the groups. In contrast, the election of women's seats engages a more diverse set of actors. More specifically, two women from each province as well as the capital (Kigali) are elected by a joint assembly composed of members of the local councils, as well as members of the executive committee of locally based women's organisations. Thus, whereas the 'electorate' for the minority seats is limited to members of the targeted groups, organised women have only partial influence over the election of 'women representatives'.

In Tanzania, special seats are reserved for two groups: women and inhabitants of the island of Zanzibar. The reserved seats allocated to women constitute 30% of all the seats in the parliament and were adopted in 1985. These seats are filled by parties after the general election, in accordance with their proportion of the votes. The Zanzibari seats are filled by the Zanzibari House of Representatives, which appoints five of its elected members to the national parliament. Thus, special arrangements are created that overlap with the constituencies of the FPTP electoral system used in Tanzania. However, there are differences in the arrangements with regard to the extent to which they aim at integration or separation. Whereas women's special seats are filled within the realm of party organisations, by men and women, the Zanzibari arrangement is more formally concentrated in the targeted group itself, protecting the Zanzibari community by granting them guaranteed influence over national politics as well as a certain amount of self-government.

No Constituency Formation, Similar Competition and Electorate

In three remaining cases, there are no differences in the design of quotas for women and minority groups as to whether special constituencies are created and with respect to the degree of separation. No new constituencies are created for women and minorities (Hindus, Christians, Ahmadis/Parsees, and other religious minorities) in Pakistan, Burundi (in the case of Hutu and Tutsi) and Palestine (Christians). The quotas are similarly designed in terms of who elects the representatives and with whom they compete.

In Pakistan, the reserved seats for both women and minorities are selected by the political parties, in relation to the number of seats the party receives in the election. Thus, the two groups are guaranteed representation in an identical manner, and no differences whatsoever can be discerned in terms of separation or integration.

In Burundi, the Hutu and Tutsi have a history of conflict and power struggles. Instead of separation, quotas for these groups provide an example of power-sharing. Such arrangements are often of a pragmatic nature, designed to avoid conflict or ethnic division along party lines. The constitution guarantees a 60:40 split between the Hutu and Tutsi, inducing an overrepresentation of the Tutsis who constitute about 14% of the population. In practice, the arrangement means that for every three candidates on a candidate list, no more than two may be from one ethnic group. This quota is designed in the same way as the 30% candidate quota for women. No new constituencies are created; instead, Hutu and Tutsi candidates stand on the same party lists and compete against other candidates from both ethnic groups and for votes from both groups.[9]

Finally, in contrast to Pakistan and Burundi, there are some differences in the design of gender quotas and quotas for the Christian minority in Palestine. Palestine has a mixed election system and quotas for women and Christians are implemented in different parts of the mixed system. Quotas for women apply to the PR lists, with at least one of the first three candidates being a woman. The quota for Christians applies to the FPTP system: in each of six appointed constituencies, one Christian is awarded a seat according to a best-loser logic. We place Palestine in this group for two reasons. First, when designing the quotas, no new constituencies were created for either women or minorities. Second, within their constituencies, both women and Christians compete with candidates and are elected by constituents from other groups (men and Muslims, respectively).

Conclusion

This article explores the underlying motives for ensuring the political inclusion of marginalised groups. More specifically, it analyses whether laws guaranteeing representation are designed differently for women and minorities and, if so, whether these variations correspond to normative arguments for group representation. When designing the empirical analysis, we contribute both theoretically and methodologically to the building of a comparative research agenda on electoral quotas for women and minorities. Methodologically, we use an improved case-selection method by including only those countries that have adopted quotas for both women and minority groups. In so doing, we can ascertain that no country-specific factors account for any possible differences in quota design between the two groups. Theoretically, we propose a novel and more relevant conceptual distinction between different types of quota designs, focusing on whether special (separate or overlapping) constituencies are created for the targeted group, or whether the quota is instead incorporated into already existing constituencies.

The empirical analysis shows that there are systematic differences in quota design between women and different minority groups. These differences do correspond to arguments put forward by normative theorists. More specifically, the overall findings suggest that the introduction of quota policies for minorities commonly rests on an underlying motive among lawmakers to recognise and separate the group in question from the ordinary electoral order. The adoption of gender quotas, on the other hand, is driven by lawmakers' aims to redistribute power by better integration of women into the existing political system (cf. Htun 2004; Kymlicka 1995).

In a majority of the cases, new, separate or overlapping, constituencies are designed for minorities but not for women. There are no instances of quotas for women being designed in a more separating manner than quotas for minorities: in none of the cases in our sample have lawmakers opted for the creation of new electoral districts for women while guaranteeing minorities representation within the existing constituencies. In addition, we show that even in those cases where new constituencies are created both for women and for minorities, the design of the constituencies is generally geared towards more separation for minorities than for women. Thus, to conclude, our analysis generally supports the suggestion that different groups receive different types of guarantees for representation.

The analysis implies that electoral quotas are not a uniform policy; to the contrary, the designs of quotas differ to a great extent also within countries. Contrary to the argument that the choice of design is dependent on the context (Krook and O'Brien 2010) or on previous experiences with a particular type of quota (Matland 2006), our analysis suggests that law-makers have different ideas about different groups in society and that these ideas affect how they design guarantees for representation for the respective groups. The perceptions of lawmakers, as they are reflected in constitutions and election laws, largely seem to corre-spond to the normative justifications for group representation put forward in the literature (Kymlicka 1995; Young 2000).

In general, policy-makers designing quotas for minority groups appear to perceive sep-aration from the dominant political actors as the priority. Quotas for minorities are designed to grant the group certain self-determination, either through the creation of special electoral dis-tricts in which only people within the group may participate (as candidates or voters) or by providing their representative institutions (organisations or assemblies) with the power to appoint representatives. Quotas for women, on the other hand, seem to be designed with their integration into the regular (s)election process in mind. Quotas for women are designed to ensure that women are elected by—and often also compete with—both men and women.

Importantly, the analysis not only provides answers; it also raises a new set of questions that future research on electoral quotas should address. For instance, the analysis draws atten-tion to the definition of 'minority quotas'. Kymlicka (1995) is mainly concerned with small ethnic minority groups who have a right to be recognised by being granted a certain amount of autonomy. When juxtaposing women with the broad category of 'minority quotas', it becomes clear that the diversity within the latter category is large and that all groups concerned with the quota cannot be considered minorities (e.g., Hutu in Burundi), even less *ethnic* minorities (e.g., youth, workers, disabled and army officials in Uganda). Future research in this emerging field should unpack the minority group further. Potential avenues for doing this include distinguishing between, on the one hand, the relation between the size of the group in question and the size of the quota and, on the other hand, between group identities that are ascribed and permanent—such as sex, ethnic or reli-gious identities—and other identities that are acquired during the course of life – such as being a young person, a worker or an army official.

In order to continue the building of a comparative research agenda on electoral quotas, we call on researchers to continue theorising and empirically examining when, how and why quotas are included in constitutions or election laws to guarantee represen-tation for specific groups in society. Case studies of the type of countries that are investi-gated in this analysis—i.e., countries with quotas for both women and minority groups—are particularly useful. Scrutinising the intentions and ideas of lawmakers when they are in the process of simultaneously designing quotas for women and minorities would contribute to a deeper understanding of the motives underpinning quota design. In addition, research-ers should carefully assess the potentially far-reaching consequences of different quota designs for women and minorities, for instance on legislative activities, to get a comprehen-sive understanding of their similar and different long-term effects, respectively. In that endeavour, we hope that our proposed new distinction of different quota types will be a useful conceptual tool.

ACKNOWLEDGEMENTS

This article is based on work supported by the Swedish Research Council (grant number 421-2010-1638). The authors thank Mona Lena Krook, Alan Renwick, Jessika Wide, Emelie

Lilliefeldt, Eleonora Stolt, Drude Dahlerup, Lenita Freidenvall, Christina Alnevall, Cecilia Josefsson, Iris Nguyen Duy, Ludvig Beckman, Petra Meier, Susan Franceschet, Thomas L. Brunell and Malin Holm for helpful comments and suggestions. The authors are equal contributors to this article: names are listed in alphabetical order.

NOTES

1. We define electoral quotas as affirmative action measures that establish a percentage or number of candidates or representatives of a specific group (see also Dahlerup 2007).

2. It should be noted that these normative arguments generally do not address more pragmatic reasons for including specific groups, such as power-sharing arrangements put in place to stabilise a divided society that has suffered from intra-state conflicts (cf. Krook and O'Brien 2010; Lijphart 1977).

3. Burundi appears twice in the analysis because it has two different sets of quota designs for different minorities.

4. We use Krook and O'Brien (2010) to identify the countries and territories. However, we exclude three countries: Tibet due to lack of information, and Belgium and Bosnia because their minority quota is only for the upper house.

5. In one case, Jordan, we also approached the IFES Country Director of Jordan, Darren Nance, for further consultation. This was done by email on 2 June 2011.

6. Taiwan also includes its expatriate community in the electoral process, but does not guarantee their representation as such.

7. The Jordanian system for distributing seats to parliament could thus be described as being entirely quota-based. However, with Muslims constituting the vast majority of the population, the 96 seats reserved for Muslims are generally not referred to as a quota.

8. The comparison between gender quotas and quotas for Hutus and Tutsis are elaborated below.

9. The Election Commission has the right to appoint members of parliament to ensure that either of the stipulated quotas is filled. This option only marginally changes the representation. Following the election of 2010, there were 100 elected and six appointed members. Three of the appointees were Twa, and the remaining three consisted of one male Hutu representative and one male and one female Tutsi representative.

References

BACCHI, CAROL. 1999. *Women, Policy and Politics*. London: Sage.

BIRD, KAREN. 2014. Ethnic quotas and ethnic representation worldwide. *International Political Science Review* 35 (1): 12–26.

DAHLERUP, DRUDE (ed.). 2006. *Women, Quotas and Politics*. London: Routledge.

DAHLERUP, DRUDE. 2007. Electoral gender quotas: between equality of opportunity and equality of result. *Representation* 43 (2): 73–92.

FRANCESCHET, SUSAN, MONA LENA KROOK and JENNIFER M. PISCOPO. (eds). 2012. *The Impact of Gender Quotas*. New York: Oxford University Press.

FRASER, NANCY. 1995. From redistribution to recognition? Dilemmas of justice in a 'post-socialist' age. *New Left Review* 212. Available at http://newleftreview.org/I/212/nancy-fraser-from-redistribution-to-recognition-dilemmas-of-justice-in-a-post-socialist-age.

HTUN, MALA. 2004. Is gender like ethnicity? The political representation of identity groups. *Perspectives on Politics* 2 (3): 439–458.

HTUN, MALA and JUAN PABLO OSSA. 2013. Political inclusion of marginalized groups. *Politics, Groups, and Identities* 1 (1): 4–25.

HUGHES, MELANIE M. 2011. Intersectionality, quotas, and minority women's political representation worldwide. *American Political Science Review* 105 (3): 604–20.

IFES (INTERNATIONAL FOUNDATION FOR ELECTORAL SYSTEMS). 2013. *Election Guide: Democracy Assistance and Election News*, available at www.electionguide.org, accessed 13 November 2013.

IPU (INTER-PARLIAMENTARY UNION). 2013. *PARLINE: Database on National Parliaments*, available at www.ipu.org/parline/, accessed 13 November 2013.

KROOK, MONA LENA. 2009. *Quotas for Women in Politics: Gender and Candidate Selection Reform Worldwide*. New York: Oxford University Press.

KROOK, MONA LENA and DIANA Z. O'BRIEN. 2010. The politics of group representation: quotas for women and minorities worldwide. *Comparative Politics* 42 (3): 253–272.

KROOK, MONA LENA. 2014. Electoral gender quotas: a conceptual analysis. *Comparative Political Studies* 47 (9): 1268–93.

KYMLICKA, WILL. 1995. *Multicultural Citizenship: A Liberal Theory of Minority Rights*. Oxford: Oxford University Press.

LIJPHART, AREND. 1977. *Democracy in Plural Societies: A Comparative Exploration*. New Haven, CT: Yale University Press.

LUBLIN, DAVID and MATTHEW WRIGHT. 2013. Engineering inclusion: assessing the effects of pro-minority representation policies. *Electoral Studies* 32 (4): 746–755.

MANSBRIDGE, JANE. 1999. Should blacks represent blacks and women represent women? A contingent 'yes'. *The Journal of Politics* 61 (3): 628–57.

MATLAND, RICHARD E. 2006. Electoral quotas: frequency and efficiency. In *Women, Quotas and Politics*, edited by Drude Dahlerup. London: Routledge, pp. 275–92.

MEIER, PETRA. 2004. The mutual contagion effect of legal and party quotas: a Belgian perspective. *Party Politics* 10 (5): 583–600.

MURRAY, RAINBOW, MONA LENA KROOK and KATHERINE A. R. OPELLO. 2012. Why are gender quotas adopted? Party pragmatism and parity in France. *Political Research Quarterly* 65 (3): 529–43.

PANDE, ROHINI. 2003. Can mandated political representation increase policy influence for disadvantaged minorities? Theory and evidence from India. *The American Economic Review* 93 (4): 1132–51.

PHILLIPS, ANNE. 2005. *The Politics of Presence*. New York: Oxford University Press.

REYNOLDS, ANDREW. 2005. Reserved seats in national legislatures: a research note. *Legislative Studies Quarterly* 30 (May): 301–31.

REYNOLDS, ANDREW. 2011. *Designing Democracy in a Dangerous World*. New York: Oxford University Press.

WILLIAMS, MELISSA S. 1998. *Voice, Trust, and Memory: Marginalized Groups and the Failings of Liberal Representation*. Princeton: Princeton University Press.

YOUNG, IRIS MARION. 1989. Polity and group difference: a critique of the ideal of universal citizenship. *Ethics* 99 (2): 250–74.

YOUNG, IRIS MARION. 1990. *Justice and the Politics of Difference*. Princeton, NJ: Princeton University Press.

YOUNG, IRIS MARION. 2000. *Inclusion and Democracy*. Oxford: Oxford University Press.

FEDERALISM AND GENDER QUOTAS IN MEXICO: ANALYSING *PROPIETARIO* AND *SUPLENTE* NOMINATIONS

Fernanda Vidal Correa

Leading approaches in the literature on women's representation have studied the effects of gender quotas in their interaction with the national electoral system. Two aspects of Mexican law have been understudied thus far, but provide important insights for understanding the degree to which quotas empower women in politics. First, quota enforcement at the subnational level depends on state-level laws, which in some cases dictate partial or no enforcement at all. Second, the joint ticket system has created a two-nominee system in which two elected figures run; the first occupies the seat (propietario) while the second is elected as a substitute (suplente). Quotas in some states may apply only to suplentes, resulting in women's entrapment in substitute and powerless positions. The analysis is based on new aggregated dataset on the nomination and election of women in a sample of 12 states' elections covering the period of 1998 to 2010.

Gender quotas have been adopted in over 100 countries, making them a global trend in strategies employed by parties and governments to increase the political representation of women. This has been accompanied by a growing number of studies in comparative politics (Baldez 2004; Dahlerup 2006; Htun and Jones 2002; Krook 2009a, 2009b; Matland 2006). Emphasis has been placed on the design of quotas among different countries and the diverse effects these have had in different electoral systems. Studies on quotas have addressed different issues including whether they are compulsory or non-compulsory, whether they are embodied in the constitutional or electoral laws, or if these are only voluntary mechanisms employed by different institutions, including political parties.

Although these studies have been vital for understanding gender quotas around the globe, most work focuses on the national level, overlooking the effects of quotas at the subnational level. Yet many countries have experienced decentralisation in recent years, making this level of government an increasingly important vehicle for women's political empowerment (Kenny and Verge 2013; Vengroff et al. 2003). Further, existing research largely focuses on quotas and candidate selection as an undifferentiated process, when in many countries in Latin America and beyond, candidate nomination processes include both primary and substitute candidates. This nuance of electoral design can have important implications for quota implementation, but has not yet been addressed in a systematic or comparative fashion.

This article seeks to take research on gender quotas in a new direction by focusing in greater detail on two dimensions affecting the implementation of quotas in Mexico, where the federal structure allows the subnational governments to play an important political role and where the separate electoral laws across states work along a substantial variation in quota design and implementation at the state level. First, the article explores how federalism affects the design of gender quotas at the state level, as states can introduce their own legal regulations. Second, the article considers the impact of the joint ticket system, whereby one candidate runs for the seat (*propietario*) while the second runs as a substitute for that candidate (*suplente*). This institutional arrangement opens up the possibility that quotas in some states may apply only to the *suplente* role, resulting in women's entrapment in substitute and powerless positions.

Based on new aggregated data collected during fieldwork in 12 of the 31 states (plus the Federal District) in Mexico, the study suggests that the main gap among women nominated and elected across states can be explained by requirements later added to the quota legislation, including the application of the quota to both sets of nominations within the joint ticket nomination system. Previous studies have suggested that sanctions for non-compliance and other additional refinements to the quota are significant in terms of its efficiency in increasing the number of women elected. Dahlerup and Freidenvall discuss the adoption of rules on ranking candidates in some Latin American countries (2005) while Schwindt-Bayer shows that the absence of placement mandates or enforcement mechanisms reduces the number of seats held by women (2009). Considering these previous studies, this analysis contends that the use of such additional refinements of the quota design to secure its effectiveness is likely to result in more women being nominated and elected in Mexican state legislatures (cf. Dahlerup and Freidenvall 2005; Jones 2009; Schwindt-Bayer 2009). Finally, this research suggests that the federal system allows differences in quota policies that result in differing levels of women's representation (cf. Jones 1998; Thomas 1991; Tuschhoff 1999; Vickers 2013). In allowing different rules, in other words, federalism may facilitate or hinder gains in women's representation. The analysis conducted is based on a new aggregated dataset on the nomination and election of women in a sample of 12 Mexican states. These were selected to reflect differences across a range of socio-economic and political factors, including regional diversity and party representation.

Gender Quotas in Renewed Federalism

Democratisation in Mexico was not the result of a particular event, but of cumulative dynamic processes in which local campaigns demanded more power from national political actors. This resulted in renewed federalism that reshaped Mexican political representative institutions, affecting the role of women in politics as well. The speed of these changes varied among states. The transformation has coincided with differences in citizenship rights. Politically marginalised groups, including women, have struggled for full citizenship in some states. The differences across institutional design and policy enforcement have resulted in women facing different circumstances in their search for political representation. Federalism does not only affect women or women's issues because it shapes policy implementation (Vickers 2011) by decentralising resources or power. Federalism also generates distinct effects due to different formal and informal institutions.

Key studies have addressed the consequences of democratic liberalisation for women's involvement in politics in Mexico. Lisa Baldez (2004, 2006) focuses on the consequences of electoral laws, mainly quotas, and the descriptive representation of women since 2002. Her research concentrates on federal elections, electoral results and elected deputies' data for recent elections (2003 and 2006), as well as the interaction between primaries and the principles for the application of the quota (Baldez 2007). Using data from both candidates and elected members, she argues that the absence of legal enforcement criteria, supported by the Federal Electoral Institute in regards to the use of gender quotas, has reduced the effectiveness of the quota. Victoria Rodriguez (2003) on the other hand, uses interviews with key political actors to provide insights into what she calls the real issues women face when entering Mexican politics, including the enforcement of gendered quotas at the municipal level (1998, 2003).

However, these studies have not focused the analysis on variations in quota policies across states and possible differences regarding the representation of women in state legislatures. Although a variety of studies have focused on the analysis of women's political representation at the state level (Aragort 2004; Gonzalez and Rodriguez 2008; Pacheco 2006; Reynoso 2005; Reynoso and D'Angelo 2004, 2006; Rodriguez 2003; Vidal 2008; Ward and Rodriguez 1999; Zetterberg 2008, 2011), these analyses have utilised data from only two or three states or have focused on historical institutional analysis of the path followed for the adoption of quotas. The work of Zetterberg and Reynoso and D'Angelo stand out since they provide a substantive examination of the quota adoption at the subnational level (cf. Zetterberg 2011) and the relative impact of specific provisions on women's representation between 1991 and 2005 (cf. Reynoso and D'Angelo 2006). The limited scope in some cases and the absence of studies focused on more recent electoral processes can be explained by difficulties in finding and retrieving data at the state level. Rules regarding access to information in the states constrain the quality of the information and its access.

According to Rodriguez, in Mexico 'women have made concerted efforts to institutionalise a quota system within government and in the organisational structures and candidate lists of political parties' (2003: 174). However, variations are likely to be observed across different levels of government because gender quotas are designed and enforced by each state (see Table 1). In these circumstances, it is fair to ask if these variations affect women's representation, with their numbers being larger in states with specific quota designs. Exploring these differences in quota design is crucial for understanding the circumstances in which women's representation is undertaken at the state level in a federal system.

Gender quotas have been adopted in most of the states' electoral codes and in the Federal Code of Electoral Institutions and Procedures (COFIPE). However, variations exist and are reinforced by a Supreme Court ruling that 'local legislatures had the right and faculty to regulate the basis of functioning' (*La Jornada* 2002). This decision strengthened the federal principle of division of power in the country. The consequence of this judicial mandate can be observed in both the design and variety of quotas adopted at the state level.

First, since each state may regulate the use of quotas, there are states that until 2012 had not approved gender quotas. Second, although many states have quotas, the percentage mandated varies. Third, the quota may be applied to the proportional representation lists, to the first past the post nominations, or to both. Finally, freedom in the drafting of regulations also applies to their enforcement. In the states studied, variations were mainly in two areas: the type of candidate the quota applies too (*propietario* or *suplente*) and the quota level (Table 1). Based on these differences, it is reasonable to expect variations in the percentages of women nominated.

A general analysis reveals that there have been substantial changes from 1998 to 2012 in the percentage of women nominated. As the quota debate advanced at the national level, gender quotas were widely adopted at the state level. During the last period studied, almost all states had adopted quotas (cf. Zetterberg 2011). Between 2008 and 2012 most

TABLE 1
Gender quota laws for candidates at the federal and subnational levels

	State	Quota	Type of Candidate	PR List Positioning
Verso:				
Recto:	Federal	60% Maximum of one gender	No specification	zipping: 2 candidates of different gender for every 5
T				
	Aguascalientes	60% Maximum of one gender	*Propietario* and *Suplente*[1]	No rule
	Baja California Sur	2/3 Maximum of one gender	*Propietario* and *Suplente*	No rule
	Chiapas	70% Maximum of one gender/ parity[2]	*Propietario* and *Suplente*	zipping: at least 1 candidates of different gender for every 3[3]
	Distrito Federal	70% Maximum of one gender (FPTP), 54% Max (PR)[4]	No specification	zipping: 2 candidates of different gender for every 5
	Estado de Mexico	60% Maximum of one gender	No specification	No rule
	Jalisco	70% Maximum of one gender (PR)	No specification	70% Max. of one gender
	Nuevo Leon	None	No Quota	No rule
	Queretaro	60% Maximum of one gender	No specification	No rule
	Sonora	Respect parity principle	No Quota	Parity without sanctions
	Veracruz	70% Maximum of one gender	*Propietario*	zipping: at least 1 candidates of different gender for every 3
	Yucatan	70% Maximum of one gender	*Propietario* and *Suplente*	From the first 3 candidates 1 of different gender
	Zacatecas	70% Maximum of one gender	*Propietario* and *Suplente*	block of 3 people with a maximum of 2 of the same gender

Source: Electoral Codes for the States of Aguascalientes, Baja California Sur, Chiapas, DF, Estado de Mexico, Jalisco, Nuevo Leon, Queretaro, Sonora, Veracruz, Yucatan and Zacatecas. Details on the quota and implementation gathered through the examination of state regulations, statutes, Constitutions and Electoral Codes. 1. The quota for *suplente* only applies to proportional representation nominations. 2. In 2009 the Electoral code was modify and parity was approved. 3. In 2009 the electoral reform established a 2 candidate block, one for each gender. 4. The Electoral code was modified in 2010. The new quota establishes a 60% one gender maximum nominations. In PR lists, the reform added a special consideration that included 2 spots within the first five positions.

states witnessed record numbers of women nominated over the last ten years. Additionally, the data reveals that all states have witnessed increased levels of women's representation, even without quota enforcement. The representation of women through states' congressional nominations steadily increased across the sampled states. However, the dispersion of the data remains high and the data contained in this chart includes all kinds of nominations (Table 2). As mentioned above, the double nomination system allows parties to nominate substitutes who will only take office in the case of the main candidate's absence. Thus, even if women are nominated as substitutes and elected they may not ever take a seat.

To conduct the analysis, a sample of 12 Mexican states was selected. The cases were selected to reflect differences across a range of socio-economic and political factors. Two main criteria were followed to select the cases: (1) regional diversity and (2) party representation. These criteria were selected because the sample needed to reflect the geographical conditions of the country, including its territorial extension and the socio-political differences between states that are located in different regions. Some of the data used in this analysis was available online in the state and federal electoral institutes, but most of the data employed was only available through requests for information made to the states' electoral institutions. Data for nominations prior to 2005 were accessed primarily at the offices of the States' Electoral Institutes.

The Double Nominating System: *Propietario* and *Suplente*

Previous research has shown that the percentages of women nominated does not reflect the exact share of the quota because there are several factors affecting the nomination process

TABLE 2
Women nominated for state legislatures, 1998–2012

States	1998-2001	2002-2004	2005-2007	2008-2010
Total Average	**20.8**	**29.0**	**33.4**	**35.4**
Range (high-low)	**25.1**	**21.5**	**22.5**	**22.9**
Standard Deviation	**5.6**	**6.8**	**6.7**	**4.4**
States in which the quota law applies to propietario nominations				
Average	**20.1**	**29.0**	**32.1**	**33.2**
Aguascalientes	25.9	21.4	35.2	35.2
Baja California Sur	19.8	26.2	36.5	37.5
Chiapas	16.2	19.6	22.5	25.0
Veracruz	22.2	31.7	39.7	34.7
Yucatan	17.5	34.2	21.9	37.1
Zacatecas	18.9	41.1	36.7	30.0
States in which the quota law does not apply to propietario nominations				
Average	20.2	29.9	33.8	36.6
Distrito Federal	34.6	38.4	40.7	40.6
Estado de Mexico	21.3	27.4	38.0	36.2
Jalisco	15.6	27.8	28.9	32.2
Queretaro	9.5	26.0	27.5	37.3
States with exceptions in the application of the quota*				
Nuevo Leon	-	24.4	28.8	31.4
Sonora	27.2	30.1	44.4	47.9

Source: Data gathered from visits to Electoral Offices in each State and freedom of information requests to State Electoral Institutes and State Electoral Courts. Data includes *propietario* and *suplente* nominations. All figures are based on the total number of candidates PAN, PRI and PRD presented. No data was available for Nuevo Leon between 1998 and 2001. * In Sonora the law requires parity and in Nuevo Leon quotas do not apply.

and quota enforcement (Htun and Jones 2002; Jones 1996, 2004; Schwindt-Bayer 2005, 2009). Dahlerup contends that 'gender quotas may produce positive effects if they are properly implemented, having the potential to increase women's representation rapidly' (2006: 19). Several factors may trump the actual effectiveness of the quota, and may even be part of the design. In the case of Mexico's state level politics, these factors relate to the nomination process followed by political parties, with a direct impact on quota enforcement. As Zetterberg suggests, 'quotas alter the rules of the game within political parties, forcing party gatekeepers to nominate women. This is likely to challenge male dominance within the parties and intensify the struggles over political power and control over the political agenda' (Zetterberg 2011: 66). Thus, how parties internally interact and decide may affect women's nominations and representation at the state level (cf. Vidal 2013b).

In Mexico the electoral system was created in an environment of political instability. To avoid unoccupied seats and the institutional volatility observed in the period just after the Mexican Revolution, a solution was proposed to create two elected figures that would run on a joint ticket (Cervantes and Medina 2011). In the case that the first named could not occupy the seat or needed to vacate it, the second person would fill it. The name given to the first on the formula is the primary candidate, or *propietario*.[1] The second in the ticket is the alternate, or *suplente*. The latter has become an indispensable element in the chain of positions that have to be occupied in order to continue advancing in the party's hierarchy. Additionally, some *suplentes* are given the position of Chief of Staff of the *propietario*.

In terms of gender quotas, flexibility in institutional design allows for quotas to be applied to both types of candidates, to one, or to none. As the following evidence shows, the two-type formula has become one of the factors limiting the actual effectiveness of the quota. Some studies suggest that in federal elections where a joint ticket nomination occurs, the absence of specificities within the law requiring the application of quotas to *propietario* nominations has resulted in the nomination of most women as *suplentes* (Baldez 2007; Vidal 2008). Further studies have shown the negative consequences that this joint ticket system has had on women (Baldez 2004; Bruhn 2003; Gray 2003; Marvan and Marquez 2013). Baldez finds, for example, that 'the law proved ineffectual because it permitted the parties to comply by nominating women to alternate spots (*suplentes*) and did not stipulate a placement mandate, which meant that women were clustered in unelectable spots at the bottom of a list' (2004: 235).

Furthermore, women deputies in Mexico have expressed that being nominated as *suplente* only works as a tool for political parties to meet public expectations without actually modifying internal structures, practices and opinions towards the empowerment of women (Vidal 2013a). An example of this behaviour was observed in the 2009 federal elections with the so-called *Juanitas*.[2] Political parties replaced women *propietarios* with male *suplentes*. Political parties informally requested elected *propietario* women to resign or take a leave of absence in order for their male *suplentes* to take the seats (Notimex 2009). For this reason, women have expressed feeling more disadvantaged than men in the election process (Vidal 2013a). This demonstrated the need for gender quotas to apply to both types of nominations and to have same-gender joint tickets.

The negative effects of this nominating system have already been recognised and addressed by judges at the federal level. On 30 November 2011, the Federal Electoral Judicial Court (TEPJF) took action to prevent the possibility of such cases being repeated. The TEPJF established criteria to ensure the presence of women once elected, establishing that the nomination of *suplentes* would include a same-sex clause in order to prevent substitutions by male representatives. The effects of this change were visible in the difficult and intricate candidate selection process of the 2012 federal election. However, this ruling has no consequences for the state level nominations.

The actions of the court addressed substitutions, but did not directly modify federal rules. As a result, there is no clear mandate regarding the application of the gender quota to both types of nominations yet. Nonetheless, the actions of the court make it possible to assume that specific rules, applied to the joint ticket system, are likely to result in more women nominated in positions that would allow them to be part of the legislatures, increasing women's empowerment through presence in these institutions.

Gender Quotas: Enforcement in *Propietario* and *Suplente* Nominations

Quotas at the state level in Mexico are subject to different specifications, including whether the regulation is exclusively for proportional representation lists, whether there are sanctions such as the rejection of non-conforming slates, and how the quota applies with regard to the joint ticket system described above. Quotas at the state level may apply to *propietario* nominations. This means that if the quota share is 40%, at least 40% of the *propietario* nominees must be of a different gender. In the event that the quota also applies to *suplente* nominations, then both *propietario* and *suplente* must have at least 40% of the nominations covered by a different gender. Since only *propietario* nominations get into office when elected, it is possible to establish that a quota applied to *propietario* is likely to result in more women taking a seat in the state legislature. Thus, the key problem with this system lies in the absence of regulations on *propietario* nominees or in the presence of a norm that applies only to *suplente* nominees.

Conversely, the absence of a rule governing the application of quotas gives party elites the power to decide its application, which in some cases may dictate partial enforcement or no enforcement at all. For example, in Yucatan each party has to nominate 20 *propietario* and 15 *suplente* candidates. The quota sets a maximum of 70% nominations of the same gender in both types of nominations. Thus, each party can nominate a maximum of 14 *propietario* and 11 *suplente* same-gender candidates. In the worst-case scenario, women should be nominated in six *propietario* and four *suplente* spots from each party. If no rule existed in Yucatan, parties could comply with the 70% quota by nominating women into eight of the 11 *suplente* spots and parties would not need to nominate women as *propietarios* to meet the quota.

On the other hand, in those states where no indications exist as to whether the quota applies to both types of candidates, *suplente*-only nominees may fill the share of the quota. For example, in Queretaro each party can nominate 25 *propietario* and 25 *suplente* candidates. From these, the quota sets a maximum 60% of same-gender nominations. This means that each party has the right to nominate, from the total of 50 (both *suplente* and *propietario*), a maximum of 30 candidates of the same gender. In the worst-case scenario, 20 nominees should be women. However, nominating 20 *suplente* women would conform to the legal requirements. Thus, women are not needed in *propietario* spots to fulfil the quota. If the quota was applied to both, then parties in Queretaro would require at least ten women nominated as *propietarios* to comply. Taking these differences into account, the study finds that six states within the sample fully apply the quota (see Table 2). This means that the quota share is expected to be reflected in both *propietario* and *suplente* nominations. In the state of Aguascalientes there is an exception. The rule establishes that the quota in *suplente* nominations should apply only in the case of proportional representation. However, the most significant application of the quota is enforced, since it is applied to *propietario* nominations in the proportional representation and in the first-past-the-post tiers. The same occurs in the case of Veracruz, where the quota share is enforced in *propietario* nominations only.

A general review of the data (see Table 3) suggests that *suplente* nominations increase in parallel with *propietario* nominations. However, women are largely nominated as *suplente*. In some cases, *suplente* women account for more than 50% of the total women nominated. It is necessary to consider whether the states that do not have a distinction in the application of the quota (enforcing it in both types of nominations) are nominating more women as *suplente*. This would suggest that even with the application of the quota, in the absence of other legal mechanisms that force parties' compliance, parties still restrict women's access to actual seats in the state legislatures.

Initially, during the first period (1998–2002) more women were nominated as *suplente* than as *propietario* across all states. States with left-wing majorities, such as Distrito Federal and Zacatecas, are key exceptions. In these two, the number of women nominated as *propietario* increased and was higher than the number of women nominated as *suplente*. Women in all other investigated states were relegated to *suplente* nominations. The overall evidence shows that women are nominated as *suplentes* equally across all the states regardless of the

TABLE 3
Women nominated as *propietario* and *suplente* between 1998 and 2010

	1998-2001		2002-2004		2005-2007		2008-2010	
	Propietario[1] (%)	Suplente[2] (%)	Propietario[1] (%)	Suplente[2] (%)	Propietario[1] (%)	Suplente[2] (%)	Propietario[1] (%)	Suplente[2] (%)
States in which the quota law applies to propietario nominations								
Average	**17.2**	**25.4**	**22.6**	**33.5**	**23.3**	**40.8**	**29.8**	**40.6**
Range	**7.3**	**20.0**	**20.1**	**27.0**	**17.5**	**30.5**	**27.3**	**14.6**
Standard Deviation	**2.4**	**7.7**	**8.4**	**11.4**	**5.9**	**11.9**	**9.0**	**6.0**
Aguascalientes	16.1	34.6	14.3	28.6	24.7	45.7	26	44.4
Baja California Sur	17.5	22.2	17.5	22.2	31.3	41.7	27.1	47.9
Chiapas	14	14.6	18.3	20.8	13.8	31.3	18.3	34.2
Veracruz	17.8	26.7	19.3	44	26.7	52.7	30	39.3
Yucatan	21.3	33.3	32	37.8	21.3	22.2	31.7	44.4
Zacatecas	16.7	21.2	34.4	47.8	22.2	51.1	45.6	33.3
States in which the quota law does not apply to propietario nominations								
Average	**12.3**	**24.5**	**12.5**	**28.2**	**16.4**	**40.3**	**22.6**	**40.0**
Range	**26.8**	**30.8**	**14.9**	**19**	**31.8**	**27.8**	**34**	**38.3**
Standard Deviation	**11.8**	**14.0**	**6.9**	**9.0**	**13.7**	**12.6**	**14.1**	**17.8**
Distrito Federal	29.3	40	11.1	24.2	31.8	49.5	41.5	39.6
Estado de Mexico	10.7	32	18.2	36.5	22	46.5	20.1	52.2
Jalisco	2.5	9.2	3.3	17.5	0	21.7	7.5	15
Queretaro	6.7	16.7	17.3	34.7	11.6	43.5	21.3	53.3

Source: Data gathered from visits to Electoral Offices in each State and freedom of information requests to State Electoral Institutes and State Electoral Courts. 1. Women's percentage from the total number of candidates nominated as propietario. 2. Women's percentage from the total number of candidates nominated as suplentes.

extra mechanisms for the enforcement of the quota. Women's nominations as *suplentes* have increased over time. In almost all cases women hold more than 30% of the *suplente* nominations. There are even cases such as Estado de Mexico and Queretaro where women have more than 50% of the total *suplente* nominations. This explains the gap between the percentage of nominations and the percentage of women who actually gain seats in the state legislatures (see Table 4).

Conversely, the nomination of women as *propietario* varies among states. Ever since quotas began to be introduced across the states[3] (cf. Zetterberg 2011: 58), those states studied with specific rulings on its application in both types of nominations outperformed states with no legal specifications. In the 2005–07 period, the average percentage difference between states was 6.96%, increasing to 7.14% in the last electoral period studied. In the period of 2008 to 2012, almost all states that have enforced the quota in the two types of candidacies have above 20% of the total *propietario* nominations filled by women. In the states without legal specifications, women only achieve an average of 15% of *propietario* nominations. Some states lag behind, i.e. Jalisco and Queretaro and Estado de Mexico.

Although the percentage difference is less than 10% between states with and without specifications on the use of the quota in *propietario* nominations, the implications of the gap among the groups is important. Previous studies have found that the adoption, modifications and transformations of quotas gives momentum to people for pushing for even deeper transformations (cf. Zetterberg 2011). Furthermore, Reynoso and D'Angelo (2006) show that in Mexican state legislatures, the presence of women in previous terms, even in small numbers, is a significant contributor to the presence of women in future legislatures (2006), bringing as well 'a new mentality among women' (Zetterberg 2011: 67). In this analysis, as the dataset shows, women's presence is increasing, either nominated (refer to Table 3) or elected. For example, in the states of Aguascalientes, Yucatan and Zacatecas, all states with specific regulations, the number of women required by the quota as *propietario* was exceeded. However, in states like Jalisco and Estado de Mexico incremental changes can be observed too, although in less robust numbers.

TABLE 4
Percentage of women elected to state legislatures, 2002–04 and 2005–07

	Women elected 2002-2004 (%)	Women elected 2007-2010 (%)
Total Average	**20.4**	**23.7**
States in which the quota law applies to propietario nominations		
Average	20.6	24.8
Aguascalientes	14.8	16
Baja California Sur	26.3	27.8
Chiapas	13.9	19.4
Veracruz	27.1	28.6
Yucatan	20	21.7
Zacatecas	21.7	35.3
States in which the quota law does not apply to propietario nominations		
Average	19	17.1
Distrito Federal	33.3	24.2
Estado de Mexico	16.7	8
Jalisco	12.2	20
Queretaro	13.6	16
States with exceptions in the application of the quota		
Nuevo Leon	26.2	22.5
Sonora	13.3	30

Source: Data gathered from visits to Electoral Offices in each State and freedom of information requests to State Electoral Institutes and State Electoral Courts. The calculation shows the percentage of women elected from the total of elected deputies. The first period comprehends election that took place between 2002 and 2004. The second period includes elections between 2007 and 2010. In the first period no quotas were enforced while in the second in some states quotas did not apply to *propietario* nominations, including Distrito Federal, Estado de Mexico, Jalisco and Queretaro. In Sonora the law stablished the need to respect parity and in Nuevo Leon quotas do not apply.

The changes have been substantial since 1998. Table 3 shows that in 1998 more women were nominated as *suplente*. When quotas were enforced, the percentage change between the 1998–2001 and the 2005–07 periods was more than 15%. Thus, even with specifications on the law regarding gender quotas, women are still largely nominated to these secondary positions. Although this situation is discouraging, it is important to look at the changes in the *propietario* nominations. On average, women occupied 15.3% of *propietario* nominations between 1998 and 2001. By 2012 the percentage increased by 11.6%. From the available 1033 *propietario* nominations (based on the number of seats in congress and the nominations made by the three main parties), between 1998 and 2001, 158 women were *propietario*. Between 2008 and 2010 the number increased and 278 women were nominated to this type of position.

Women nominated in states with specific regulations regarding the position type have fewer women nominated as *suplentes,* with a percentage difference from those without regulations of 6.6%. The difference in *propietario* nominees is smaller, with a percentage difference of 2.25% between 1998 and 2002 and 2008–10. As quota regulations were tightened, differences between states with and without regulations on *propietario* nominees became more

TABLE 5
Percentage change in women elected to state legislatures, 2002 to 2010

Percentage change 2002-2010.	
States in which the quota law applies to propietario nominations	
Average	**4.2**
Aguascalientes	1.2
Baja California Sur	1.5
Chiapas	5.5
Veracruz	1.5
Yucatan	1.7
Zacatecas	13.6
States in which the quota law does not apply to propietario nominations	
Average	**-1.9**
Distrito Federal	-9.1
Estado de Mexico	-8.7
Jalisco	7.8
Queretaro	2.4
States with exceptions in the application of the quota	
Nuevo Leon	-3.7
Sonora	16.7

Source: Data gathered from visits to Electoral Offices in each State and freedom of information requests to State Electoral Institutes and State Electoral Courts. The calculation shows the percentage of women elected from the total of elected deputies. The first period comprehends election that took place between 2002 and 2004. The second period includes elections netween 2007 and 2010. In the first period no quotas were enforced while in the second in some states quotas did not apply to propietario nominations, including Distrito Federal, Estado de Mexico, Jalisco and Queretaro. In Sonora the law stablished the need to respect parity and in Nuevo Leon quotas do not apply.

visible. Political parties in states with regulations nominated on average 23.33% women as *propietario,* while parties in states without regulations nominated 16.35%. In the same period there was no difference in the percentage of women nominated as *suplentes* between states with and without regulations.

Many factors influence the choice of certain candidates over others and therefore their subsequent election. Thus, the direct causal relationship between the number of women elected and the impact of electoral law can vary significantly across cases and time. Notwithstanding, it is possible to note that norms like legal regulations, electoral rules and systems of party competition controlling the construction of the pool of eligibles can have significant effects on the profile of the persons occupying the seats (Norris 1997). Others have found that when more women are included in the pool of candidates, the probability that women will make it onto party ballots and get elected is higher as well (Norris 1985; Oakes and Almquist 1993; Randall 1987). As stated by Schwindt-Bayer, 'more women in the candidate pool leads to more women in office' (2009: 20).

For example, between 2002–04 and 2005–07, in all states with specific regulations for the application of quotas in *propietario* nominations, the percentage of elected women increased steadily (Table 4). The comparison between the two periods is significant because in the first, quotas were not applied, and in the second, they were enforced along with *propietario* specifications. Among those states with and without regulations there are differences in the pool of *propietario* nominees but the main difference is observed in the percentage of women elected. Since the adoption of quotas, within the group of states with regulations a positive trend can be observed. On the other hand, states without regulations show erratic be-haviour, with clear exceptions such as Distrito Federal and states with low numbers of both nominated and elected women, such as Jalisco, Queretaro and Estado de Mexico.

Finally it is important to emphasise the differences in the percentage of women elected before quotas and after their adoption. Mainly, variations occur between states with specific laws that apply to *propietario* nominations and states without specific laws but with quotas. The average percentage change rate in the states with laws is 4.15% more women elected between 2002 and 2004 and in the last electoral period. The states without specifications regarding *propietario* nominations have a negative average percentage change rate (see Table 5). For example, in Nuevo Leon, where up to the election of 2009 no quotas were applied, there was a much higher loss in the percentage of women elected. Sonora, on the other hand, is the only state within the sample that includes in its regulations parity between women and men, and it experienced an increase of 16 points. It is clear that more specific rules in the application of quotas are having positive results in Mexico.

It is necessary to emphasise that the quota share in most states was never completely attained, regardless of the party in power. In most cases, the quota was avoided using a legal loophole embedded in the quota design, internal primaries. In the law, when the nomi-nation is the outcome of an internal process, parties are allowed to disregard any quota (the *voto directo* clause is discussed in Baldez 2007). The use of all available loopholes by political parties is a clear symptom of the parties' willingness to nominate women. Thus, the use and design of quotas still plays a role in getting women elected in Mexican state legislatures.

Conclusions

Quotas have been perceived as a fast track or 'a kick-start for women to gain entry to politics . . . or to prevent a backlash' (Dahlerup and Freidenvall 2005: 143). However, these have not generated an automatic increase in elected women. In fact, as this study has demon-strated, in spite of quotas, women's representation has remained low in Mexico. The possibi-lities of variations permitted by the federal system have made the presence or absence of gender quotas not the only element that needs to be considered or studied. The evidence pre-sented here is consistent with other findings. Research where interviews are conducted revealed the difficulties of overcoming discrimination against women embedded in the use of *suplente* nominations (Vidal 2013a).

Based on previous research on sanctions for non-compliance, placement mandates and additional refinements to the quota design, greater differences were expected. Although some differences between those states where the law applies to *propietarios* and where it does not can be found in the women nominated as *propietario* and in the women holding office, there is perhaps room for some nuance. Other things may be identified here than the quota design. In the Mexican case, due to the design of the electoral system, in which the majority votes are counted for the proportional representation seats distribution, parties are using women who are accepted in the community to pose as *suplente* candidates in order to attract more votes (Rodriguez 2003; Vidal 2013a). The willingness of the parties to enforce the quota and nominate women as *propietario* is controversial. As discussed above, the behaviour of the party towards women may help explain isolated differences across states. Thus, quota design may explain some of the differences but perhaps not all of them and further studies should explore this. The evidence has shown that the existing Mexican legislation should contemplate a specific clarification regarding the enforcement of quotas on *propietario* nominations. Parties largely comply with the quota by nominating women for *suplentes* positions, which ultimately limits women's real empowerment.

The existing specifications for the enforcement of quotas are important in terms of the quota efficacy, measured by the increase in the number of women elected. When quotas were first introduced, small differences in their design could lead to the nomination or isolation of women in non-eligible positions, such as *suplentes*. Data shows that in the period of 2005 to 2007, when quotas accompanied by penalties for lack of enforcement at the local level were introduced, specifications within the norms were important for securing the nomination of women as *propietario*. As time has passed and women are gaining their own political weight, states with and without rules are showing similar results. This does not imply that quotas can now be abandoned. Women in state legislatures are gaining more access but in many cases they still do not hold even 15% of the seats. Thus, the small differences between states with and without specific norms in the percentage of women nominated as *propietario* are likely to continue being significant for the improvement of women's representation across the state.

Further research on the effectiveness of gender quotas should thus focus further on their design and implementation mechanisms. Additionally, future research should not only focus on cross-national variations, but also differences within individual countries, especially those organised as federal systems. This study of Mexican states points to such variations. In some states, the quota helped but did not guarantee the nomination of women, indicating a fruitful new research agenda for exploring favourable quota designs.

ACKNOWLEDGEMENTS

This work was conducted with support from the Institute for Legal Research (IIJ) of the National Autonomous University of Mexico (UNAM) and the General Directorate of Academic Staff and Affairs (DGAPA). The study was part of doctoral research carried out at the Department of Politics at the University of Sheffield (UK). Alistair McMillan's guidance and the valuable comments of Mona Lena Krook and Pär Zetterberg led to significant improvements in this article, although all responsibility for the content is exclusively mine. The participation of women deputies and senators across the different states is also recognised and appreciated.

NOTES

1. The joint ticket applies to the election of city trustees, local deputies, federal deputies and senators. Usually, the elected *propietario* will serve the complete term. The second in the formula usually takes office only when someone wants to run for office in the following election. According to Mexican electoral laws, subsequent re-election is forbidden but people can run for a different position. In this case, the person has to take leave of absence some time before the election. The time of the leave varies according to the position sought.

2. Initially, the term was used to make reference to the ten federal deputies, eight of them women, that after two days of having been sworn as deputies, requested leave of absence,

making way for the *suplentes* candidates, who were men. Moreover, the men that got the seats were related to these women. Some were siblings or husbands. After this case, the term was employed to refer to women who left their seats either by pressure from the party or by their own will, to their male *suplentes*.

3.   By 2006 almost all states had adopted quotas. In the case of all states in the sample, those with quotas had enforced them since the third period studied.

REFERENCES

ARAGORT, YUBIRI. 2004. La democratización en los espacios de poder local y el clientelismo político Parroquia Osuna Rodríguez. *FERMENTIM* 0274: 533–60.

BALDEZ, LISA. 2004. Elected bodies: the gender quota law for legislative candidates in Mexico. *Legislative Studies Quarterly* 29 (2): 231–58.

BALDEZ, LISA. 2006. The pros and cons of gender quota laws: what happens when you kick men out and let women in? *Politics & Gender* 2 (1): 102–28.

BALDEZ, LISA. 2007. Primaries vs. quotas: gender and candidate nominations in Mexico, 2003. *Latin American Politics & Society* 49 (3): 69–96.

BRUHN, KATHLEEN. 2003. Whores and lesbians: political activism, party strategies, and gender quotas in Mexico. *Electoral Studies* 22 (1): 101–19.

CERVANTES, IRINA and ALDO MEDINA. 2011. Los retos de la justicia constitucional electoral local en México. *Revista de Estudios Constitucionales* 3 (1): 15–24.

DAHLERUP, DRUDE (ed.). 2006. *Women, Quotas and Politics*. London: Routledge.

DAHLERUP, DRUDE and LENITA FREIDENVALL. 2005. Quotas as a 'fast track' to equal representation for women: why Scandinavia is no longer the model. *International Feminist Journal of Politics* 7 (1): 26–48.

GONZALEZ, MARIA LUISA and PATRICIA RODRIGUEZ. 2008. Obstaculos y Limitaciones en el empoderamiento de las mujeres: la experiencia del PRD. In *Limites y Desigualdades en el empoderamiento de las mujeres en el PAN, PRI y PRD*, edited by Maria Luisa Gonzalez and Patria Rodriguez. Mexico: Miguel Angel Porrua, pp. 175–202.

GRAY, TRICIA. 2003. Electoral gender quotas: lessons from Argentina and Chile. *Bulletin of Latin American Research* 22 (12): 52–78.

HTUN, MALA and MARK JONES. 2002. Engendering the right to participate in decision-making: electoral quotas and women's leadership in Latin America. In *Gender and the Politics of Rights and Democracy in Latin America*, edited by Nikki Craske and Maxine Molyneux. Hampshire: Palgrave Macmillan, pp. 32–56.

JONES, MARK. 1996. Increasing women's representation via gender quotas. *Women & Politics* 16 (4): 75–98.

JONES, MARK. 1998. Gender quotas, electoral laws, and the election of women: lessons from the Argentine provinces. *Comparative Political Studies* 31 (1): 3–21.

JONES, MARK. 2004. Quota legislation and the election of women: learning from the Costa Rican experience. *The Journal of Politics* 66 (4): 1203–23.

JONES, MARK. 2009. Gender quotas, electoral laws, and the election of women evidence from the Latin American vanguard. *Comparative Political Studies* 42 (1): 56–81.

KENNY, MERYL and TANIA VERGE. 2013. Decentralization, political parties, and women's representation: evidence from Spain and Britain. *Publius: The Journal of Federalism* 43 (1): 109–28.

KROOK, MONA. 2009a. Beyond supply and demand: a feminist-institutionalist theory of candidate selection. *Political Research Quarterly* 63 (4): 707–20.

KROOK, MONA. 2009b. *Quotas for Women in Politics: Gender and Candidate Selection Reform Worldwide.* New York: Oxford University Press.

LA JORNADA. 2002. La Ley de cuotas de género de Coahuila, no es inconstitucional como planteó el PAN: SCJN. 4 March, available at http://www.jornada.unam.mx/2002/03/04/arts_43/43_cuotas.htm, accessed 18 June 2010.

MARVAN, MARIA and LOURDES MARQUEZ (eds). 2013. *Democracia interna de los partidos vs. cuotas de género, ¿dilema sin solución?.* IFE: Mexico.

MATLAND, RITCHARD. 2006. Electoral quotas: frequency and effectiveness. In Women, Quotas and Politics, edited by Drude Dahlerup. London: Routledge, pp. 275–92.

NORRIS, PIPPA. 1985. Women's legislative participation in Western Europe. *West European Politics* 8 (4): 90–101.

NORRIS, PIPPA (ed.). 1997. *Passages to Power: Legislative Recruitment in Advanced Democracies.* Cambridge: Cambridge University Press.

NOTIMEX. 2009. Permanente otorga licencias a siete Juanitas. 22 December. Available at http://www.eluniversal.com.mx/notas/647492.html, accessed 21 August 2010.

OAKES, ANNE and ELIZABETH ALMQUIST. 1993. Women in national legislatures. *Population Research and Policy Review* 12 (1): 71–81.

PACHECO, LOURDES. 2006. Sistemas de cuotas y agendas de género en Baja California Sur, Coahuila, Colima, Durango, Guerrero, Jalisco y Nayarit. Introducción. In *La cuota de género en México y su impacto en los Congresos Estatales. Baja California Sur, Colima, Coahuila, Durango, Jalisco, Guerrero y Nayarit,* edited by Claudia Cervantes. Tepic: Universidad Autónoma de Nayarit, pp. 11–48.

RANDALL, VICKY. 1987. *Women and Politics: An International Perspective.* Chicago: University of Chicago Press.

REYNOSO, DIEGO. 2005. Competición Electoral y Des-hegemonizacióon en los Estados Mexicanos. In Despues de la alternancia: Elecciones y nueva competitividad, edited by Victor Espinoza and Rionda Ramirez. EL Colegio de la Frontera Norte y Sociedad Mexicana de Estudios Electorales, pp. 165–95.

REYNOSO, DIEGO and NATALIA D'ANGELO. 2004. Leyes de Cuotas y Elección de Mujeres en México ¿Contribuyen a disminuir la brecha entre elegir y ser elegida? Torreon.

REYNOSO, DIEGO and NATALIA D'ANGELO. 2006. Las leyes de cuota y su impacto en la elección de mujeres en México. *Politica y Gobierno* 13 (2): 279–313.

RODRIGUEZ, VICTORIA. 2003. *Women in Contemporary Mexican Politics.* Austin: University of Texas Press.

SCHWINDT-BAYER, LESLIE. 2005. The incumbency disadvantage and women's election to legislative office. *Electoral Studies* 24 (2): 227–44.

SCHWINDT-BAYER, LESLIE. 2009. Making quotas work: the effect of gender quota laws on the election of women. *Legislative Studies Quarterly* 34 (1): 5–28.

THOMAS, SUE. 1991. The impact of women on state legislative policies. *The Journal of Politics* 53 (4): 958–976.

TUSCHHOFF, CHRISTIAN. 1999. The compounding effect: the impact of federalism on the concept of representation. *West European Politics* 22 (2): 16–33.

VENGROFF, RICHARD, ZSOLT NYIRI and MELISSA FUGIERO. 2003. Electoral system and gender representation in sub-national legislatures: is there a national—sub-national gender gap? *Political Research Quarterly* 56 (2): 163–73.

VICKERS, JILL. 2011. Gender and state architectures: the impact of governance structures on women's politics. *Politics & Gender* 7 (2): 254–62.

VICKERS, JILL. 2013. Is federalism gendered? Incorporating gender into studies of federalism. *Publius: The Journal of Federalism* 42 (3): 1–23.

VIDAL, FERNANDA. 2008. El papel de la mujer en la conformacion del aparato gubernamental: una mirada a partir de las reformas electorales en materia de equidad de genero. In *Limites y Desigualdades en el empoderamiento de las mujeres en el PAN, PRI y PRD*, edited by Maria Luisa Gonzalez and Patricia Rodriguez. Mexico: Miguel Angel Porrua, pp. 63–76.

VIDAL, FERNANDA. 2013a. Women's representation in Mexican state politics. PhD thesis, University of Sheffield, Department of Politics.

VIDAL, FERNANDA. 2013b. La descentralización de los procesos de selección de candidatos en los partidos y su impacto en la nominación de mujeres en los Congresos Estatales de México. *Revista Mexicana de Ciencias Políticas y Sociales* 58 (217): 171–95.

WARD, PETER and VICTORIA RODRIGUEZ. 1999. New federalism, intra-governmental relations and co-governance in Mexico. *Journal of Latin American Studies* 31 (3): 673–710.

ZETTERBERG, PAR. 2008. The downside of gender quotas? Institutional constraints on women in Mexican state legislatures. *Parliamentary Affairs* 61 (3): 442–60.

ZETTERBERG, PAR. 2011. The diffusion of sub-national gender quotas in Mexico and their impacts. In *Diffusion of Gender Quotas in Latin America and Beyond*, edited by Adriana Piatti-Crocker. New York: Peter Lang, pp. 53–69.

GENDER QUOTAS AND 'WOMEN-FRIENDLY' CANDIDATE SELECTION: EVIDENCE FROM BELGIUM

Audrey Vandeleene

Belgium is one of the world leaders with regard to gender quotas, with strict rules for gender parity being imposed on political parties. Nonetheless the question remains as to whether these requirements for gender-equal list formation have led to women-friendly candidate selection procedures. Noting a gap in research on this topic, this article proposes a definition of 'women-friendly' candidate selection procedures and then analyses nine Belgian political parties along two axes: who is in charge of selections and how the selection process is organised. Using data from interviews as well as party statutes, the article seeks to explore the broader meaning of gender quotas for candidate selection processes, above and beyond increasing women's representation in parliament.

Introduction

'Women are not better, but different'. This assertion from a female politician reflects the struggle for equal representation of women and men in politics. Since women's representation in parliament is filtered through the mechanism of party electoral lists, candidate selection assumes a central role in shaping gender equality in this regard. Selection processes can vary a lot across parties, and while some features may be favourable towards female candidates, others might disadvantage women.

Belgian politics is known for becoming increasingly 'women-friendly' (Meier 2012). Far-reaching legislation has been adopted in order to impose parity on electoral lists. Yet political parties still differ in terms of share of female candidates heading a list, ranging in 2007 from none to two-thirds. Starting from this large variation between parties, this article seeks to understand the cross-partisan differences by examining the ways in which candidate selection procedures shape women's possibilities to be nominated and—at the end of the day – elected.

Noting that there is little literature that tackles the impact of features of candidate selection processes on women's presence on safe spots, the article proposes an analysis along two dimensions directly related to the process in itself. The first concerns the characteristics of selectorates, with the existing literature suggesting that the degree of inclusiveness and centralisation may affect women's presence. The second axis involves the degrees of complexity and institutionalisation in candidate selection processes. The main argument put forward is that the introduction of gender quotas does not necessarily lead candidate selection procedures to become more 'women-friendly'.

Seeking to chart a new direction in quota research, the article seeks to explore whether the introduction of new candidate selection requirements has an impact on the openness of political parties towards women candidates. The empirical analysis mobilises both textual and interview data from the nine main Belgian political parties in 2007, combining party statutes and representation statistics with perceptions of key political actors regarding the feminisation of Belgian politics. The article shows notably that the presence of gender quotas for selectorates matters for an increased number of female candidates on top spots.

A gendered approach to candidate selection through the eyes of political parties

Political parties are the gatekeepers on the road to an elected assembly (Caul 1999; Cross 2008; Norris and Lovenduski 1995; Wiliarty 2010). Through candidate selection processes parties reduce the pool of aspirants into a pool of candidates (Matland and Montgomery 2003). As a result, in most countries without support from a party, no aspirant can be elected.

Consequently, the internal life of political parties must be studied in order to understand women's presence in politics (Baer 1993). Parties are the pivotal actors explaining barriers to increased female representation (Franceschet 2005), as well as the effectiveness of quotas in increasing women's presence (Murray 2010). As Krook (2009b) argues, the onus for change lies with political elites, due to the power and discretion they enjoy when selecting candidates.

Candidate selection is indeed a critical step in an election, since selection procedures partly determine the composition of elected assemblies (Rahat 2007). Some seats can always be considered safe for some parties, such that by choosing who will be put where, parties in effect choose which individuals will most certainly be in office during the next legislature. From a gender perspective, therefore, parties hold the power to more or less ensure equal representation in parliament in those particular seats. Only marginal seats would be subject to the election results. If those other candidacies are equally distributed, then parity in parliament is more or less guaranteed.

One way to encourage parties to pursue parity in candidate nominations is to introduce electoral quotas. Quotas force parties to select a certain proportion of female candidates. From the 1970s onwards, quotas have spread all over the world, starting from Europe and then South America (Krook 2009a). Legislative quotas in particular require parties to adapt their candidate selection procedures in order to recruit more women. Because of this forced political renewal, some male candidates have had to step aside, leaving their place to new female candidates (Murray 2010). Yet some view quotas as undemocratic since they privilege the latter over the former, who may not be qualified (Krook 2009b). Such constraining mechanisms aiming at fairer representation can significantly impact candidate selection processes. But parties remain free to decide how they will put such requirements into practice, leaving room for a wide range of possible interpretations.

Hypotheses

It has been argued that work on political parties suffers from gender blindness (Murray 2010). Yet cross-fertilisation is promising. The concept of gender can help to better understand what happens inside political parties. To this end, this article develops and tests several hypotheses regarding the women-friendliness of candidate nomination procedures. Two key dimensions are identified: characteristics of selectorates and of the selection process.

Selectorates, or party bodies that select candidates (Rahat and Hazan 2001), are often defined along two axes: the degree of inclusiveness, or how large the selectorate is, and the degree of centralisation, or how close it is to the national level.

In terms of its size, a selectorate can take multiple forms (Hazan and Rahat 2010). On one end of the spectrum, the party elites—a single leader or a small group of selectors—can select candidates. On the other end, party rank-and-file members can participate in the process. In some parties the voters themselves are called to vote through open primaries. Between these two extremes, different formulas exist such as list committees, party agencies specially constituted to select candidates, and delegate conferences.

The inclusiveness of the selectorate can have a number of effects on the outcomes of the candidate selection process (Field and Siavelis 2008). The literature suggests that inclusive selectorates may prevent parties from ensuring the representation of specific social groups within the pool of candidates (Rahat 2007). Stated in another way, it appears easier for a more exclusive selectorate, as opposed to a more inclusive one, to ensure that enough women are present in winnable spots. A large assembly of delegates or a poll among party provides fewer guarantees in this respect.

H1: A more exclusive selectorate encourages women-friendliness in selection.

The extent to which selectorates are close to the national level of the party also matters (Hazan and Rahat 2010; Lovenduski and Norris 1993). Territorial centralisation is maximal when decisions are taken from one place for the whole party. Conversely the selection is decentralised when the lower instances of the party play a role at the constituency or local level.

Research suggests that the degree of territorial centralisation also has an impact on a party's ability to guarantee parity (Norris 1997; Rahat 2007). Control over the selection process from above ensures that the party has a broad overview of who is running for election. In contrast, decentralised selectorates can select candidates without thinking beyond their own constituencies, which may lead to fewer women being put forward. Caul Kittilson (2006) has shown that centralised parties are more likely to offer women more opportunities because the party leadership can be held more directly accountable for a lack of women-friendliness.

H2: A more centralised selectorate encourages women-friendliness in selection.

Beyond size and level of centralisation, the mere composition of the selectorate may have an impact on propensity towards women-friendliness. The outgroup effect theory explains why this may be important (Niven 1998; Tremblay and Pelletier 2001). Members of selectorates consider themselves as part of the ingroup. They evaluate outgroup members negatively, judging good candidates to be those who share their same characteristics. Out-group members aspiring to office may therefore benefit from having people like them as part of the selectorate in order to increase their chances of being selected. The gender composition of the party top (Caul Kittilson 2006) and of selectorates in particular (Cheng and Tavits 2011) may then matter for more gender equal outcomes. Gender quotas guaranteeing a proportion of women within selectorates may thus increase women's chances of being selected as candidates.

H3: Gender quotas for selectorates encourage women-friendliness in selection.

In addition to variations in the composition of selectorates, candidate selection processes may vary in terms of their institutionalisation and complexity. Candidate selection processes entail both formal and informal practices (Krook 2009a). Party rules may strictly specify how to conduct the selection process and who intervenes, but many parties also rely on party habits and traditions. Various systems exist, ranging from the most institutionalised, whereby everything is standardised and explicit, to the least institutionalised, where actors enjoy more discretion and freedom (Norris and Lovenduski 1995).

Candidate selection procedures are also subject to varying degrees of complexity. Assorted and multistage candidate selection methods are distinguished by Hazan and Rahat (2010). The method is assorted when different selectorates select candidates, or when different rules apply for certain types of candidates, for example heads of list. As a result, the party ends up with a set of candidates who do not come from the same selection process. A method is multistage when the process involves distinct selectorates who select the same candidates at successive points in time.

Institutionalisation and complexity may affect the ease with which women gain access to the lists. The more institutionalised the selection process, the easier it is for outsiders to the party to understand which steps take place when and which actors play a role (Czudnowzski 1975; Norris and Lovenduski 1995). If the whole process is well detailed in party documents, newcomers—such as most women—are more likely to get an opportunity to participate. Transparency is crucial, as opaque procedures favour insiders that are familiar to it. However, work by Caul (1999) finds that parties with low levels of institutionalisation tend to have gender-related rules, even if one might expect the opposite.

H4a: Institutionalised processes encourage women-friendliness in selection.

The interaction between complexity and institutionalisation may affect the process' accessibility for newcomers like women. A complex selection process, but highly institutionalised, would not discriminate outsiders since they would be able to grasp the complexity through consulting written rules. However, if the process is complex and informal, only aspirants well-acquainted with these dynamics are in the position to get into the selection process. The final hypothesis is therefore that complexity in itself is not problematic, but the non-institutionalisation of complex processes narrows access for outsiders.

H4b: Non-institutionalised complex processes discourage women-friendliness in selection.

Data and method

The research is based on two main types of data, which complement one other. The first involves textual data from the statutes of the nine main Belgian political parties, which is used in order to describe the formal aspects of candidate selection processes.[1] The second entails in-depth interviews with Belgian key political actors, which are qualitatively analysed to gain a more in-depth view of candidate selection procedures in practice.[2] The interviews focused on the recruitment and selection of candidates for eligible mandates, as well as for internal party positions. The individuals interviewed in each party included one person from the party president's inner circle; one expert situated high up in the internal organisation of the party, usually the national secretary; one woman active within the party, typically the women's section president; and one complementary person, in most cases an MP. The transcripts of all interviews were analysed with a computer assisted qualitative data analysis software (QSR NVivo).

Gender and Candidate Selection in Belgium

Belgium is classified as a parliamentary democracy having a proportional representation electoral system with semi-closed lists. Voters can either vote for the entire list, meaning that they agree with the order chosen by the party, or they can specify particular candidates on that list by casting a preference vote. Candidates are elected according to the D'Hondt system. As a result, the higher a candidate is situated on a list, the more chances s/he has to be elected, unless s/he wins a large number of preference votes, enabling him or her to bypass candidates placed higher on the list. Despite the presence of this mechanism, the order of the candidates on the lists remains very important for getting elected (De Winter and Dumont 2000), meaning that political parties still play a very central and powerful in determining who is elected.

Belgian political parties face few regulations when drawing up their lists. Apart from some general rules,[3] almost everyone can become a candidate (Banneux 2012). The most constraining rule relates to gender quotas. The first quota law was passed in 1994 and forced parties to have no more than two-thirds of candidates of the same sex on the lists. Nowadays parties have to respect the 2002 gender quota act stipulating that on each list the difference between the numbers of candidates of each sex must not be more than one. Moreover the two top candidates on each list cannot be of the same sex. This legislation has produced substantial effects at the federal level only since 2007 because of several transitory measures containing weaker obligations.[4] Legal quotas have had a dramatic effect on Belgian politics (Mateo Diaz 2002), increasing women's share of parliamentary seats from less than 10% in 1995 to nearly 40% by 2014.

Nine parties fall within the scope of this research. The Belgian political system is divided in two, whereby Flemings and Francophones live under the same legislative system and follow the same electoral rules but function as two parallel worlds (Billiet et al. 2006). Political parties split apart in the late 1960s and 1970s (Dandoy and De Decker 2009) and now operate relatively independently in Flanders and in Wallonia with some overlap in the Brussels Capital Region. Additionally, ideological differences also exist. Among the nine analysed parties, four are considered leftist (Ecolo, Groen!, PS and sp.a), two are situated in the centre (cdH and CD&V), and three are rightist, among which two are liberal (MR and Open Vld) and one is on the far right (VB).[5]

Even though they are required to respect the same quota laws, parties differ regarding the proportion of women in their ranks, as shown in Table 1. Three groups can be distinguished based upon women's share of the lists.[6] Only figures for electable[7] places are presented, since parity is mandatory for the lists as a whole. The top spot on the list is also taken into account, given that parties are indeed forced to allocate either the first or the second place to a woman.

TABLE 1
Share of women on electoral lists (Belgian political parties, 2007)

Political party	% women on electable spots	% women heading a list
Ecolo	50.0	66.7
sp.a	60.8	33.3
Groen!	50.0	33.3
PS	40.0	16.7
MR	45.8	16.7
cdH	37.5	33.3
CD&V	36.4	16.7
Open Vld	36.0	16.7
VB	33.3	0.0

It is on the winnable positions and in top spot where parties can demonstrate their women-friendliness, or not.

Three parties reached or exceeded the threshold of having equal numbers of women and men in the eligible places their lists: sp.a, Ecolo and Groen! Moreover, these parties entrusted the top place on the list to a female candidate in two-thirds (Ecolo) or one-third (sp.a and Groen!) of their lists. A second group of parties placed women in 40% of their winnable spots and one sixth of the top places (PS). MR did slightly better in terms of placing women in electable positions (45.8%) but a bit worse when it came to the very top of the list (16.7%). The last group includes four parties selecting less than 40% women in safe seats and placing women as the head of the list one time out of three (cdH), out of six (CD&V, Open Vld) or not at all (VB).

Analysis

Intuitively, one would expect that parties giving a greater place to female candidates on their electoral lists would provide a closer fit with the profile of women-friendly candidate selection processes sketched above. This section compares women's presence on party lists with the features and rules identified above as being more 'women-friendly', drawing on the materials from the parties' statutes.

Who Selects?

The size of the selectorate and its degree of centralisation may affect how a party treats female candidates during the selection process. I first explore whether parties with more exclusive selectorates score better in terms of women's positions on the lists. Three types of selectorates found in Belgian political parties include party rank-and-file members, delegates selected by members, and party leaders. Figure 1 shows interestingly that in the great majority of parties, more than one kind of selectorate plays a role in the selection process.

The results do not match with the expectations in the existing literature. The MR has the most exclusive selectorate and gives only average chances to women on its lists. The sp.a and the VB have a slightly less exclusive selectorate but are totally opposite in their approaches to selecting women. Ecolo, CD&V, Open Vld and PS have all quite inclusive selectorates—both

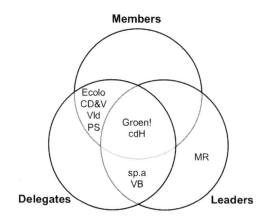

FIGURE 1
Degree of inclusiveness of selectorates

members and delegates participate in the process—but differ with respect to women's presence on lists. Finally, Groen! and cdH have the most inclusive selectorates, but again reflect distinct inclinations when it comes to placing women in winnable positions.

In terms of the degree of centralisation, it was hypothesised that centralised selectorates—close to the national level—should lead to larger proportions of women in safe seats. As shown in Figure 2, two parties (CD&V and Open Vld) have decentralised selectorates and nominate lower proportions of women on the top of their lists. One party (VB) selects its candidates in a quite centralised manner and also has high numbers of women in electable positions. The rest of the parties, however, do not fit with the expected pattern. The hypothesis does not find a perfect match in the Belgian data.

Nevertheless, data from the interviewees highlight the need for central control in order to guarantee women's presence on the lists. Keeping the whole picture in mind, in terms of candidate nominations across the country, is crucial because—as one interviewee said—if only men are in the top positions, the party can just as well elect no female MPs. In Groen!, some constituencies are compelled by the central party to put a woman on the top spot. Proactive support for women is thus exercised top-down. A Green reports that she has proposed that the party put female candidates on the head of list in half of the constituencies, but this regulation is not in force because of respect for local autonomy.

Although localised candidate selection has not generally been women-friendly, a female interviewee noted that the local section has had to change its mentality as a consequence of legal quotas. 'Previously, men made these decisions among themselves while drinking beer'. This very frustrating situation for women has changed after the quota act, she reported, because men now felt obliged to accept women. She asserted that local sections were still the most chauvinist structures; they would require more time to feminise and modernise because they are far more conservative than the party at the national level. In short, the interviewees' statements align with arguments in the literature, but the data on candidate selection across the political parties do not entirely confirm these insights.

The third hypothesis relates to the composition of the bodies selecting candidates. It has been argued that if selectorates are representative in terms of gender, it is more likely that the outcome will be women-friendly. The relevance of studying quotas for selectorates was

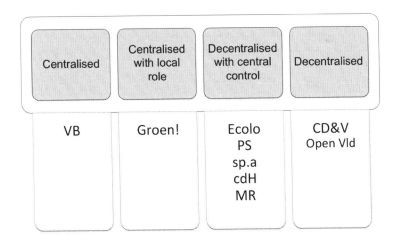

FIGURE 2
Degree of centralisation of selectorates

emphasised by respondents. Selectorates' composition in terms of gender is an influencing factor, in the words of a Christian-Democrat. A male interviewee asserted that when a selecting body was only constituted by men, there might be a tendency to select only men as well.

As result, women's sections in many parties try to be represented among the selectorate. As an interviewee pointed out, women's sections need to be attentive to this point since there is no legislation mandating their participation. Furthermore, having more than a single representation is crucial as the quantity of women may be decisive for the outcome. Women's sections are also important to contact female party members to ensure their presence at general member polls, where only physically present members can vote.

Another interviewee suggested that if only men were selectors, they would select only particular kinds of women. For instance, an older male politician might choose a young woman who is young, trendy and attractive—and who they see as not endangering their own power. Nevertheless, even if a balanced selectorate might be expected to select more women, it is important to point out that not all men are anti-women by definition; indeed, some may be more gender-friendly than some women.

Table 2 shows the selectorates for all parties, categorised according to the three main steps of the drawing-up process. In most parties in Belgium, these roles are fulfilled by different selectorates. *Proposition* refers to the moment when selectorates make the first draft of the list (the so-called model list), *evocation* is an in-between step when some selectorates hold a some sort of veto right, and *adoption* is when selectorates give their final approval to the list. Gender quotas or requirements for a specific selectorate are indicated in pale grey. General gender quotas applying for all party bodies are in dark grey.

Some parties apply specific quotas for some selectorates, which sometimes go further than the quota applied to all party bodies. Ecolo imposes a one-third quota within its federation council, a delegates' conference organ that holds the power to reject a list and make it restart from scratch. Groen! sets a one-third quota within delegates being part of the national political board. This body holds the last word regarding electoral lists. Delegates within PS party board must not be more than four-fifths from the same sex. This quota is quite superfluous because the general party quota for bodies is one-third and delegates form the vast majority of the board. CD&V's constituency boards must respect a one-third quota within regional delegates. Additionally, the board presidency has a 50% quota. cdH's constituency special committees also have to respect a one-third quota within the presidency. Four parties, finally, provide an 'expansion rule' which entails expanding the body's composition in order to reach the quota if this is not respected in the initial composition.

In addition to these quota requirements, some selectorates must be composed of a certain number of members of the party women's section. One delegate from the women's section can sit in two sp.a bodies (with a consultative voice) and within the cdH national political board. Finally CD&V reserves some seats to delegates from its women's section within all constituency boards and within the general assembly.

In terms of groups, parties from the top group of parties respecting gender parity (Ecolo, sp.a, Groen) all have gender regulations but these are not as constraining as other parties. The two parties from the second group behave in a diametrically opposite manner. PS imposes a one-third quota for all selectorates while MR has established no gender quota. As for the third group, they are separated in two: the Christian-Democrats impose a gender quota, whereas Open Vld and VB hardly regulate the composition of their selectorates. In sum, there are parties that slightly fall short or surpass expectations, but all parties with high numbers of women in winnable positions have some type of quotas for their selectorates.

TABLE 2
Selectorates' types and role and gender quotas

	Proposition	Evocation	Adoption
Ecolo	Constituency list committee	Federation council (delegates)	Constituency assembly (members)
	Parity as a goal	1/3	
	Parity as a goal in all bodies		
Groen!	National poll committee		Poll (members) AND National party board
			1/3 within delegates
	Parity as a goal in all bodies		
PS	(sub)constituency committee	Party board	(sub)constituency congress AND Poll (members)
		1/5 within delegates	
	1/3 mandatory and parity as a goal in all bodies (expansion if necessary)		
sp.a	Constituency board	Party board	Constituency congress
		One WS delegate (consultative)	One WS delegate (consultative)
	1/4 mandatory and parity as a goal in all bodies (expansion if necessary)		
cdH	Constituency special committee	National political board	Poll (members)
	1/3 within the presidency	One WS delegate	
	1/3 mandatory and parity as a goal in all bodies (expansion if necessary)		
CD&V	Constituency board AND general assembly	General assembly (delegates)	Poll (members)
	1/2 within the presidency; 1/3 within regional delegates; 3 WS delegates	5 WS delegates; WS staff (consultative)	
	1/3 mandatory and parity as a goal + WS presence (expansion if necessary)		
MR	Electoral commission AND Head of list		Electoral commission
	No gender quota		
Open Vld	Constituency working group AND Constituency board		Poll (members)
	Parity as a goal in all bodies		
VB	Party board		Party council
	No gender quota		

How Do They Select?

In addition to the actors involved, the interaction between the degree of complexity and institutionalisation of the selection process is expected to influence the nomination of female candidates. As hypothesised above, a complex but institutionalised selection process would not disfavour women, whereas a complex but non-institutionalised process would be a disadvantage. But institutionalisation alone also plays a role, with the literature suggesting that non-institutionalised processes favour insiders, more formal processes do not necessarily disfavour outsiders. The nine parties are classified in Figure 3 according to both of these dimensions.

Two parties have quite complex and formal selection procedures. Ecolo and Groen! select their candidates through a multistage and 'assorted' process, i.e., candidates are not all selected in the same way. Candidates on winnable or strategic places[8] are selected by more centralised selectorates than candidates for other places on the list. The interaction between complexity and institutionalisation is crucial for these parties. Because their procedures are complex, an informal selection process would disfavour women. This is not the case because both have formal rules regulating how candidates must be selected. These parties have, in addition to their statutes, a specific document containing all the details of these procedures. The hypothesis is totally confirmed in these parties, given their high numbers of electable female candidates.

sp.a, cdH, CD&V and Open Vld also have formal procedures. In the statutes of these four parties, the process of candidate selection is detailed, either in a specific chapter or in several articles. Their selection process is less complex than in the two green parties because it is multi-stage but not assorted. Yet it stays quite complex, with three or more steps. The sp.a meets the expectations of the hypothesis, given its high numbers of nominated women, whereas the hypothesis does not hold true for the other three parties, who have less favourable nomination patterns.

The last three parties do not specify which rules apply to the selection of candidates with as much detail as the other parties. The PS gives almost a free hand in the selection process to its more decentralised party bodies. The MR chooses the heads of the lists, but then allows these to compose the remainder of their own list themselves. The VB hardly describes the selection process in its statutes. This party was indeed expected to be informal. The other two were expected to be intermediate in their degree of institutionalisation and complexity.

Information from the interviews is nuanced regarding the effect of institutionalisation on women-friendliness. In a Green's opinion, a written profile and application can have a deterrent effect on women willingness to put themselves forward as candidates, because women often lack the required self-confidence to do so. Selectorates have then to approach candidates personally and encourage them by emphasising their qualifications. Another interviewee made a similar point, suggesting that because women are more modest, they would be less likely to spon-taneously say that they would like to become MP or minister. Selectorates have to go and con-vince women instead of letting them apply by themselves. Therefore, if the process is too formal,

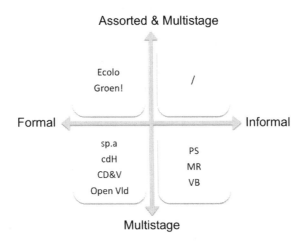

FIGURE 3
Complexity and institutionalisation of selection procedures

women's reluctance to stand could play in their disfavour. Notwithstanding these trends, a female respondent pointed out that even when list formation appears to be a formal process, informal dynamics still operate such that not everyone has the same chance to be selected.

Conclusions

Altogether Belgian political parties appear to be women-friendly, in the sense of nominating increased numbers of women. Partly as a consequence of gender quotas, no single party had in 2007 less than one-third women in the winnable positions on its lists. Yet differences still exist between the political parties, since some manage to achieve parity and others do not. This article aims to explain why some parties do better than others in terms of women's presence in the safe places. It does so by analysing whether features of candidate selection process have an impact on the openness of political parties to nominate women to these list positions.

Two dimensions of party selection processes have been tested, based on evidence from party statutes and interviews with key actors within parties. The analysis shows that the actors in charge of candidate selection can impact the likelihood of selecting women to winnable spots. The literature suggested that exclusive and centralised selectorates would favour women, although the results in this study find that this is not the case for all parties. Data from the interviews, however, highlight in particular the relevance of centralised selectorates. The potential for the national level leadership to intervene is crucial because local bodies tend to be more chauvinistic and are less able to see the larger picture to ensure equal representation across constituencies. In terms of who selects, the analysis provides quite straightforward evidence of the importance of gender quotas for selectorates: all parties with the highest numbers of women in winnable positions have gender-related rules for the bodies selecting candidates. Interviewees also pointed to the need for women to present at this level in order to ensure the selection of female candidates.

Second, the article probes the role of institutionalisation and of complexity of selection processes on the nomination of women. As expected, it appears that parties with complex but institutionalised procedures do score better than other parties.

On the whole, this research charts a new direction in quota research by delving deeper into the relationship between the structure of the candidate selection process and the prospects for women to be nominated to winnable positions on their parties' lists. This presents important insights into the larger question of what gender quotas stand for in terms of transforming not only the composition of parliament, but also in opening up candidate selection procedures to women's increased participation. A crucial finding, in particular, was that gender quotas for selectorates can play a vital role in ensuring the full implementation of gender quotas for lists. Further research should test the hypotheses on other cases to gain more definitive knowledge on which features of candidate selection might be more conducive than others to women's enhanced political representation.

ACKNOWLEDGEMENTS

Earlier versions of this article were presented at the ECPR Joint Sessions of Workshops, Mainz, March 2013 and at the ECPR General Conference, Bordeaux, September 2013. I wish to thank in particular both special issue editors, Mona Lena Krook and Pär Zetterberg, for their valuable and constructive comments on the manuscript. I also express my gratitude to Min Reuchamps and Emilie van Haute for their generous feedback on my work.

NOTES

1.	The following statutes have been analysed: Ecolo (October 2007), Groen! (18 June 2005), PS (4 March 2007), sp.a (22 November 2002), cdH (18 May 2002), CD&V (May 2005), MR (24 March 2005), Open Vld (12 October 2004), VB (2004). All were in force at the time of the 2007 federal elections, or nothing related to gender or candidate selection has been changed in the earlier version (according to contacts with party officials).
2.	These interviews, 36 in all, were conducted in 2006 by a Belgian research team supervised by Petra Meier and Benoît Rihoux (Meier et al. 2007).
3.	Such as nationality, age and not being deprived of one's civil and political rights.
4.	At the time of the first renewal of the federal parliament (2003), the first three candidates of each list had to be of a different sex.
5.	For more details on Belgian political parties' ideological positions, see Meier and Verlet (2008).
6.	All percentages concern elections to the lower house (i.e., the Chamber of Representatives) in 2007.
7.	Defined as the number of seats won by the party at the previous election
8.	Next to electable positions, which are on the top of the list, strategic places include also the last place on the list, according to Ecolo's statutes. The last candidate on the list is traditionally highly visible during the campaign.

REFERENCES

BAER, DENISE L. 1993. Political parties: the missing variable in women and politics research. *Political Research Quarterly* 46 (3): 547–76.

BANNEUX, NICOLAS. 2012. Les conditions d'éligibilité. In *Les systèmes électoraux de la Belgique*, edited by Frédéric Bouhon and Min Reuchamps. Brussels: Bruylant, pp. 173–87.

BILLIET, JAAK, BART MADDENS and ANDRÉ-PAUL FROGNIER. 2006. Does Belgium (still) exist? Differences in political culture between Flemings and Walloons. *West European Politics* 29 (5): 912–32.

CAUL, MIKI. 1999. Women's representation in parliament, the role of political parties. *Party Politics* 5 (1): 79–98.

CAUL KITTILSON, MIKI. 2006. *Challenging Parties, Changing Parliaments*. Columbus: The Ohio State University Press.

CHENG, CHRISTINE and MARGIT TAVITS. 2011. Informal influences in selecting female political candidates. *Political Research Quarterly* 64 (2): 460–71.

CROSS, WILLIAM. 2008. Democratic norms and party candidate selection: taking contextual factors into account. *Party Politics* 14 (5): 596–619.

CZUDNOWZSKI, MOSHE. 1975. Political recruitment. In *Handbook of Political Science: Micropolitical Theory*, vol. 2, edited by Fred Greenstein and Nelson Polsby. Boston, MA: Addison Wesley, pp. 155–242.

DANDOY, RÉGIS and NICOLAS DE DECKER. 2009. Peut-on encore parler de 'partis frères' en Belgique? In *L'absence de partis nationaux: menace ou opportunité?*, edited by Jean-Benoit Pilet, Jean-Michel De Waele and Serge Jaumain. Brussels: Ed. de l'ULB, pp. 19–35.

DE WINTER, LIEVEN and PATRICK DUMONT. 2000. PPGs in Belgium: subjects of partitocratic dominion. In *Parliamentary Party Groups in European Democracies: Political Parties behind Closed Doors*, edited by Knut Heider and Ruud Koole. London: Routledge, pp. 106–29.

FIELD, BONNIE N. and PETER M. SIAVELIS. 2008. Candidate selection procedures in transitional polities: a research note. *Party Politics* 14 (5): 620–39.

FRANCESCHET, SUSAN. 2005. *Women and Politics in Chile*. Boulder, CO: Lynne Rienner.

HAZAN, REUVEN Y. and GIDEON RAHAT. 2010. *Democracy within Parties: Candidate Selection Methods and Their Political Consequences*. Oxford: Oxford University Press.

KROOK, MONA L. 2009a. *Quotas for Women in Politics: Gender and Candidate Selection Reform Worldwide*. Oxford: Oxford University Press.

KROOK, MONA L. 2009b. The diffusion of electoral reform: gender quotas in global perspective. Paper presented at the 37th ECPR Joint Sessions of Workshops, Lisbon, 14–19 April.

LOVENDUSKI, JONI and PIPPA NORRIS. 1993. *Gender and Party Politics*. Thousand Oaks, CA: Sage.

MATEO DIAZ, MERCEDES. 2002. Are women in parliament representing women? From descriptive to substantive representation . . . And back again? Doctoral dissertation, Université catholique de Louvain.

MATLAND, RICHARD E. and KATHLEEN A. MONTGOMERY. 2003. *Women's Access to Political Power in Post-Communist Europe*. Oxford: Oxford University Press.

MEIER, PETRA. 2012. From laggard to leader: explaining the Belgian gender quotas and parity clause. *West European Politics* 35 (2): 362–79.

MEIER, PETRA and DRIES VERLET. 2008. La position des femmes en politique locale belge et l'impact des quotas. *Swiss Political Science Review* 14 (4): 715–40.

MEIER, PETRA, BENOÎT RIHOUX, SILVIA ERZEEL, ANOUK LLOREN and VIRGINIE VAN INGELGOM. 2007. *Partis belges et égalité de sexe, une évolution lente mais sûre?* Brussels: Institut pour l'égalité des femmes et des hommes.

MURRAY, RAINBOW. 2010. *Parties, Gender Quotas and Candidate Selection in France*. London: Palgrave Macmillan.

NIVEN, DAVID. 1998. Party elites and women candidates: the shape of bias. *Women and Politics* 19 (2): 57–80.

NORRIS, PIPPA. 1997. *Passages to Power: Legislative Recruitment in Advanced Democracies*. Cambridge: Cambridge University Press.

NORRIS, PIPPA and JONI LOVENDUSKI. 1995. *Political Recruitment: Gender, Race and Class in the British Parliament*. Cambridge: Cambridge University Press.

RAHAT, GIDEON. 2007. Candidate selection: the choice before the choice. *Journal of Democracy* 18 (1): 157–70.

RAHAT, GIDEON and REUVEN Y. HAZAN. 2001. Candidate selection methods: an analytical framework. *Party Politics* 7 (3): 297–322.

TREMBLAY, MANON and RÉJEAN PELLETIER. 2001. More women constituency party presidents: a strategy for increasing the number of women candidates in Canada? *Party Politics* 7 (2): 157–90.

WILIARTY, SARAH E. 2010. *The CDU and the Politics of Gender in Germany: Bringing Women to the Party*. Cambridge: Cambridge University Press.

THE EFFECTIVENESS OF QUOTAS: VERTICAL AND HORIZONTAL DISCRIMINATION IN SPAIN

Pablo Oñate

The electoral quota passed in Spain in March 2007 stipulated at least 40% candidates of either sex for all elected offices. Seeking to explore how effective this measure has been in generating conditions of political equality in a broader sense, this article analyses the degree to which this regulation has resulted in a rise in the number of female MPs, as well as to their presence in leading positions and their nomination to a wide range of parliamentary committees. Comparing trends in 18 national and regional legislatures before and after the quota was introduced, the analysis concludes that the quota led to a modest increase in the numbers of women elected, but did little to reduce vertical and horizontal segregation or bridge the gap between nominations to traditionally 'feminine' and 'masculine' portfolios.

Introduction

Electoral quotas are nowadays a common element of many democratic systems. In the last two decades voluntary or legal measures have been approved in many democracies, although they have had variable outcomes (Dahlerup 2006; Jones 2005; Krook 2009; Zetterberg 2008). Overall, the proportion of female representatives is still low in many countries, including some with gender quotas, with the world average now standing at 22.3% (Inter-Parliamentary Union 2014). Growing evidence suggests, however, that the presence of female MPs in descriptive terms (Pitkin 1967) has achieved better representation in substantive terms, as well as a change in the style of politics (see Childs and Krook 2006; Swers 2002).

Today there is a positive attitude towards gender parity in the international arena, complemented by widespread mobilisation at the national level. This pressure has had a contagious effect on political parties, whose leaders have embraced parity due to a perceived risk of losing votes if they do not (Escobar-Lemmon and Taylor-Robinson 2005; Krook and O'Brien 2012; Krook and Norris 2014; Paxton et al. 2006).[1] As a result, electoral quotas have become quite common and have positively influenced the increase of female MPs in many national and regional legislatures (Paxton et al. 2010). An associated change has been an increase in the gender-friendly policies proposed in many democratic systems (Franceschet and Piscopo 2008).

Nevertheless, the increase in the number of women in politics in the last decades does not necessarily entail a change in the gendered distribution of power in terms of gains in top leadership positions (vertical discrimination) (Krook and O'Brien 2012; Paxton et al. 2010; Studlar and Moncrief 1999). At the same time, when women have won political positions, they 'have largely been relegated to the least powerful positions', being allocated often to cabinet portfolios and parliamentary committees defined as 'feminine' and those with less prestige (horizontal discrimination) (Krook and O'Brien 2012: 840; also Darcy 1996; Davis 2007; Escobar-Lemmon and Taylor-Robinson 2005; Heath et al. 2005; Studlar and Moncrief 1999). For these reasons, it is important to analyse not only the increase of the number of female representatives in a given polity (the 'quantity' of women), but also the degree to which their greater presence leads to the erosion of traditional patterns of vertical and horizontal segregation.

In this article I address these issues by examining the effects of Spain's 'Act for the Effective Equality of Women and Men' that was passed in 2007. This law establishes an electoral quota for all elected offices: electoral lists for any election—at the national, regional or local level—are required to have at least 40% candidates of each sex, in every five positions on the party list as well as on the list as a whole. Some parties had previously approved voluntary quotas, and some regional governments had passed legal quotas, which together led to an increase in the numbers of female MPs in the respective regional legislatures.[2] The article analyses the effectiveness of the 2007 legislative quota in increasing women's numbers, as well as in reducing levels of vertical and horizontal segregation, using data from the national lower chamber, the Congreso de los Diputados, and the 17 regional legislatures.

First, I analyse the effectiveness in terms of quantity, comparing the evolution of the percentages of female MPs across two sets of elections, before and after the 2007 Act was passed, at both the national and regional level.[3] Next, I analyse the impact of the quota on vertical segregation, gauged according to the allocation of female MPs to leadership positions within the legislatures, including president, presidency board and board of parliamentary party speakers. Third, I analyse the presence of female MPs in leadership positions on parliamentary committees, both before and after the quota was passed. Finally, in order to analyse the impact on the horizontal segregation, I aggregate the committees according to whether they have traditionally been seen as 'feminine' or 'masculine', with the aim of seeing whether female MPs are evenly distributed among them. The empirical analysis I used compared descriptive statistics on data from 18 legislatures: in 2007, they encompassed 1564 MPs, 301 committees, 981 committee presidency board positions, and 4969 committee seats. Data were gathered from the legislatures' websites.

The analysis sheds light on the broader impact of electoral quotas, at least in the short run, in terms of their ability to enact a broader transformation of power within the political sphere. The study indicates that, first, the 2007 legal quota was quite effective in terms of increasing the number of women in parliament, even if it did not achieve the election of 40% women everywhere, although it should be acknowledged that these changes were part of an ongoing trend initiated in the 1990s. Second, these gains have not been as positive in relation to the distribution of male and female MPs in leadership positions within each legislature and its committees. Third, considerable gaps still exist between the types of committees to which male and female MPs are allocated. My conclusion is therefore that while quotas may be effective instruments in increasing women's numbers, they are not sufficient in and of themselves to tackle problems of vertical and horizontal discrimination in representative institutions.

The Impact of Quotas on the Proportion of Female MPs in Spanish Legislatures

The presence of female MPs in Spain has evolved dramatically over the last 30 years (Figure 1). After the first democratic elections in 1977, only 6% of the national MPs were

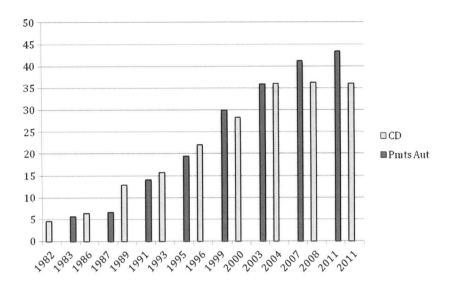

FIGURE 1
Evolution of the presence of female MPs in Spain (in %)
Source: Oñate (2011: data from legislatures' websites).
 CD: Congreso de los Diputados (National Lower Chamber).
 Pmts Aut: regional legislatures.

women. By 2004, this figure had risen to 36.3%, placing Spain among the top ten countries in the world in terms of female MPs. It was the only non-Scandinavian country, together with Rwanda, in these leading positions (Kittilson 2006; Christmas-Best and Kjaer 2007). Thus, a substantial increase in the number of female MPs took place prior to the adoption of the 2007 quota law. The main driver was a contagion effect across the political parties, whereby the adoption of party quotas—most notably in the Socialist Party—leading other political parties to take steps to increase the presence of female candidates on their electoral lists. Regional legal quotas and international pressure also played an important role (Serra 2011; Threlfall 2007; Verge 2006).

The 2007 legal quota generalised the requirement of at least 40% female candidates on every party list for the Congreso de los Diputados and the regional legislatures. The impact of this quota in the Congreso de los Diputados was quite small: the increase was only 0.3% in the number of female MPs, similar to election results in 2004 and 2008. The impact was greater across the 2003 and 2007 regional parliaments, as shown in Table 1. Overall, the law had a positive impact, even if there were slightly different outcomes in each region. There was a reduction of the number of female MPs in only two legislatures, but notably in both cases the resulting percentages were still above the quota requirement, due in part to the earlier presence of regional legal quotas. In the regional legislature of Murcia, the number of female MPs remained the same and below the legal quota. In all, women's representation reached 40% in 12 out of the 17 regional legislatures.

The quota was not respected equally by all the parliamentary political parties in each legislature (see Table 2). Several common trends are worth mentioning. First, the Socialist Party registers the highest percentages of female MPs across all the legislatures, exceeding the 40% quota in the Congreso de los Diputados and in 15 out of the 17 regional legislatures. Despite its 45.3% average across the regional parliaments, however, there is as much as an

TABLE 1
Female MPs in Spanish legislatures (in %)

	2004	**2008**
Congreso de los Diputados	**36.0**	**36.3**
Regional parliaments	2003	2007
Andalusia	29.5	45.0
Aragon	31.3	32.8
Asturias	31.1	44.4
Balearic Islands	37.5	44.0
Canary Islands	35.0	38.2
Cantabria	41.0	43.6
Castile-La Mancha	53.2	46.8
Castile-Leon	36.0	41.0
Catalonia	29.6	38.5
Extremadura	36.9	43.1
Galicia	33.3	40.0
La Rioja	39.4	42.4
Madrid	37.8	48.3
Murcia	31.1	31.1
Navarra	32.0	34.0
Basque Country	52.0	45.3
Valencia	41.6	46.4

Source: Oñate (2011); data taken from legislatures' websites.

TABLE 2
Female MPs in parliamentary parties (in % of party's seats) 2007 and 2008

	Legislature	PSOE	PP	IU	CiU	PNV	CC	ERC	BNG	PAR
Congreso Diputados	36.3	41.0	32.2	50.0	40.0	0.0	50.0	0.0	50.0	0.0
Andalusia	45.0	48.2	46.8	0.0						
Aragon	32.8	36.7	34.8	0.0						22.2
Asturias	44.4	47.6	35.0	50.0						
Balearic Islands	44.0	45.0	46.4							
Canary Islands	38.2	46.2	40.0				42.1			
Cantabria	43.6	50.0	41.2							
Castile-La Mancha	46.8	50.0	42.9							
Castile-Leon	41.0	42.4	41.7							
Catalonia	38.5	45.9	35.7	41.7	37.5			33.3		
Extremadura	43.1	44.7	40.7							
Galicia	40.0	44.0	34.0						50.0	
La Rioja	42.4	50.0	41.2							
Madrid	48.3	45.2	47.8	45.5						
Murcia	31.1	33.3	32.1	0.0						
Navarra	34.0	41.7	31.8	50.0						
Basque Country	45.3	48.0	38.5	0.0		53.3				
Valencia	46.4	51.4	41.5	50.0						
Mean regional legislatures	41.6	45.3	39.5	26.4						

Source: Oñate 2011 (with data from Legislatures' websites). (*) The number of seats of the parties in Congreso de los Diputados beyond PSOE's and PP's ones are too small to even analyze their percentage of female MPs. IU usually has very few seats in the regional legislatures, so it's percentages are to be taken carefully.

18-point gap across the different legislatures. The Popular Party has lower figures of female MPs, with 39.5% on average and with more than 40% in only 10 out of the 17 regional legislatures, with a 16-point gap across different legislatures. These data confirm for Spain the general theory that left-wing parties tend to have higher percentages of female MPs (Escobar-Lemmon and Taylor-Robinson 2005; Krook and O'Brien 2012). Among the non-state-wide parties (CiU, PNV, CC, ERC, BNG, PAR) there are also wide variations that do not indicate any clear pattern, although they tend to have high levels of female MPs in their regional parliamentary groups.

The Impact of Quotas on Membership in Governing and Leadership Bodies

Going beyond the numbers, the analysis next maps the share of female MPs holding leadership positions in each legislature. Political party groups are very hierarchical in Spain, with the leadership tightly controlling most of the activity in each chamber (Oñate 2000, 2008; Oñate and Delgado 2006). Appointments for presidency board positions, both in the legislature and in the committees, are determined by the leadership of the two parties winning the most seats, but especially the winning party.

The number of female chamber presidents was relatively high prior to 2007, when the quota was passed: 40% of the 18 legislatures had a female president in 2003–04, a figure rising to 50% in the legislatures governed by a regional quota system (Table 3). Regarding the presidency board[4] within each legislature, whose composition is negotiated among the leaders of the larger parliamentary parties, there are wide variations among legislatures in terms of the number of female members, without a clear relation to the number of female

TABLE 3
Female presence in the governing bodies of the legislatures

	Female Legislature President		Female members of the Presidency Board (%)		Female members of Parliamentary Party Speakers Board (%)	
	2003	2007	2003	2007	2003	2007
Congreso Diputados	0	0	33.3	33.3	11.1	28.6
Andalusia	1	1	37.5	50.0	50.0	45.5
Aragon	0	1	40.0	60.0	0.0	0.0
Asturias	1	1	20.0	60.0	37.5	37.5
Balearic Islands	0	1	0.0	40.0	20.0	20.0
Canary Islands	0	0	20.0	40.0	25.0	33.3
Cantabria	0	0	60.0	60.0	0.0	0.0
Castile-La Mancha	0	0	40.0	20.0	20.0	50.0
Castile-Leon	0	0	60.0	60.0	50.0	40.0
Catalonia	0	0	42.9	14.3	41.7	41.7
Extremadura	0	0	20.0	20.0	40.0	33.3
Galicia	1	1	40.0	20.0	25.0	12.5
La Rioja	0	0	40.0	40.0	16.7	20.0
Madrid	1	1	42.9	57.1	36.4	47.1
Murcia	0	0	0.0	40.0	0.0	0.0
Navarra	1	1	40.0	20.0	0.0	0.0
Basque Country	1	1	60.0	40.0	16.7	20.0
Valencia	1	1	60.0	60.0	50.0	50.0

Source: own elaboration. Data taken from legislatures' websites.

MPs in each legislature (Table 3). Taken together, the average level for the 18 parliaments rose from 36.0% to 40.6%, before and after the quota. The number of parliaments with a presidency board with at least 40% female members rose from 11 to 12, out of the 18. Only seven legislatures registered an increase in the proportion of female members on the presidency board; six had the same proportion; and five had fewer women on their boards after the quota was passed. These patterns suggest that the quota had a minimal impact in fostering a more gender-friendly attitude in allocating female MPs to leading positions.

The presence of female members in the parliamentary party speakers board (PPSB) of each legislature[5] also varies substantially among parliaments, as shown in Table 3, both before and after the quota was passed. The average percentage of women across the 18 PPSBs rose from 28.4% before the quota to 30.8% afterwards. The number of legislatures with a PPSB with at least 40% female members rose from five to six, out of the 18. Four legislatures, however, had no female members in their PPSB. The proportion of women in these bodies increased in only six parliaments, while it remained the same in eight and diminished in four. These data again show that the impact of the quota in diminishing gender discrimination in the legislatures' governing and leading bodies was small.

The Impact of Quotas on the Assignments to Committees and Committee Governing Bodies

Committee assignments within the legislatures are decided by the leaders of the respective parliamentary parties, usually respecting the requests of each MP. The incentives for each MP to be assigned to one or the other committee are different and difficult to evaluate, in most cases being a matter of personal preference. The MPs of the larger parties belong to two or three committees, but those from the small parties belong to as many as eight or ten.

It could be expected that the electoral quota might entail changes in the composition of parliamentary committees and access to leadership positions within the committees. Indeed, the number of gender-balanced committees (defined as being at least 40% female) increased following quota adoption in 2007, as shown in Table 4 (first two columns).[6] All of the observed legislatures (except one, in which the numbers are still quite high) increased the number of committees with at least 40% female MPs. Nevertheless, they are still far from having all their committees gender-balanced: eight of the legislatures do not reach gender balance in even half of their committees, and only two legislatures do so at least in 75% of their committees. The evidence indicates remarkably big differences between legislatures in this respect, variations that cannot be explained in terms of governing party or other common variables. Taken all together, slightly more than half (53.8%) of the 301 analysed committees for 2007 are gender-balanced in their composition, compared to 46.3% in the legislatures elected in 2003. Thus, even if the presence of female MPs in the committees has increased, there is still more work to be done to achieve a gender-balanced distribution of female MPs in all of the committees.

There are also big differences among the 18 legislatures regarding leadership positions within committees, as shown in Table 4. The percentage of committees with a female president in each legislature increased in only six of the 11 analysed cases, while it decreased in four and remained the same in one. In five of the 18 legislatures the share of committees with female presidents did not reach 40% of the total number of committees, even if they get close to that figure. This compares to six out of 11 for which we have data in 2003. The total number of committees with a female president is 44.5% (134 out of the 301). This reflects

TABLE 4
Female MPs in the legislatures' committees

	% Committees with Women > 40%		% Committees with female President		% female MPs in Comm Presidency Board	
	2003	2007	2003	2007	2003	2007
Congreso Diputados	23.1	32.1	30.8	32.1	32.5	28.7
Andalusia	59.1	63.6	50.0	50.0	48.6	48.7
Aragon	33.3	53.8	41.7	38.5	42.1	36.6
Asturias	20.0	46.2	20.0	46.2	40.0	51.3
Balearic Islands	27.3	46.2	36.4	46.2	43.3	53.8
Canary Islands	56.3	68.8	37.5	50.0	46.0	59.1
Cantabria		61.5		38.5		43.6
Castile-La Mancha	95.0	88.9	65.0	55.6	66.7	55.6
Castile-Leon	46.7	63.2	53.3	52.6	48.9	54.2
Catalonya		39.1		47.8		37.5
Extremadura	23.5	58.8	11.8	35.3	33.3	43.1
Galicia		28.6		35.7		32.6
La Rioja	33.3	46.2	33.3	46.2	36.1	53.8
Madrid		50.0		56.3		47.9
Murcia		30.0		40.0		40.6
Navarra		37.5		43.8		42.0
Basque Country	71.4	60.0	64.3	46.7	66.7	44.7
Valencia		78.3		43.5		61.0

Note: 2003: 7 missing cases (Cantabria, Cataluña, Galicia, Madrid, Murcia, Navarra, and Valencia).
Source: own elaboration. Data taken from legislatures' websites.

an increase of 2.5% if compared to the legislatures elected in 2003, for the 11 cases for which we have data, in line with the spirit of the legal quota.

The empirical evidence also shows that the presence of female MPs in the committee presidency boards (CPB) increased after quota introduction, approximating gender-balance: in only four legislatures did female members of the CPB not obtain 40% of the positions. The aggregate level of female representation decreased, however, by 0.7 points in the 981 committee board posts across the 18 legislatures, to 45.6%. This is due to large differences across the various parliaments. But, even if gender balance was not attained in all 18 legislatures, the total figure still indicates gender balance in the committee governing positions of Spanish legislatures.

It is worth mentioning that those legislatures that had approved regional legal quotas in 2002 and 2005 (see footnote 2) are not the legislatures with the highest levels of female presence as president, members of the presidency board, or members of the board of party speakers. Additionally, it should be taken into account that in the 2007 election the Socialist Party (the strongest supporter of gender quotas) suffered a strong defeat, losing a large number of seats in all legislatures, whereas the conservative Popular Party (still opposed to electoral quotas) won the election and many seats in most of the legislatures. The increase of the numbers of women in leading positions is therefore independent of party ideology.

The Impact of Quotas on the Gendered Committee Assignments

Beyond the presence of female MPs in the leading positions in the chambers and in their committees, there is also the question of distribution, namely whether women are assigned

71

evenly across all the committees—or if they tend to be concentrated more in some committee types than others. As noted above, even if decided by her or his party leaders, committee assignments depend to a large extent on the personal preferences of the MP, not necessarily linked to her or his educational and professional background, although this can be an important factor.

Literature on parliamentary committees and cabinet ministers has classified portfolios in different ways, distinguishing between inner and outer cabinets, masculine versus feminine portfolios, and high versus low prestige assignments, classifications taking into account traditional perceptions, capacity to develop policies, size of assigned budget and personnel, and media visibility. The general finding has been that the proportion of women tends to be higher in outer cabinets and feminine and low prestige portfolios (Davis 2007; Druckman and Warwick 2005; Escobar-Lemmon and Taylor-Robinson 2005; Heath et al. 2005; Krook and O'Brien 2012; Laver and Shepsle 1994; Studlar and Moncrief 1999). After trying various specifications,[7] the analysis below focuses on 'feminine' versus 'masculine' portfolio types.

Traditionally, female MPs have tended to be concentrated to a larger extent in what were considered 'feminine committees',[8] those dealing with the private realm: health, education, social services, family, and women's affairs. In contrast, female MPs' presence has often been lower in traditionally 'masculine'[9] ones, those dealing with the public sphere: defence, economy, labour, interior, foreign affairs, and justice. Using this classification, the data on committee assignments was examined to see whether the introduction of the legal quota changed these traditional gendered distributions, opening the way for a more even distribution of MPs across all committees.

Taking all 18 legislatures together, it is a clear that the traditional pattern is still quite evident: women are still more likely to be assigned to committees dealing with traditionally 'feminine' concerns (see Table 5). Yet, interestingly, while the proportion of female MPs increased in both kinds of committees in the 2007 legislatures, the increase in assignments to traditionally 'masculine' portfolios tripled the rate for the 'feminine' ones. While the gap has diminished, it nonetheless remains quite sizeable at 13.5 points.

Horizontal discrimination is also apparent when looking at which committees have more than 40% female members. Although there is still a way to go in order to achieve gender balance in all committees, there is a marked difference by committee type. More than half of all 'feminine' committees are gender-balanced, but only about a third of 'masculine' committees are (see Table 6). The introduction of the legal quota (and its associated increase in the number of female MPs) in 2007 did not reduce this gap, which instead grew by two points compared to the pre-quota period.

TABLE 5
Female MPs in committees, by portfolio of committee (in %)

	'Feminine portfolio' committees	'Masculine portfolio' committees
2003	47.9	32.1
2007	48.8	35.3

Source: own elaboration. Data taken from legislatures' websites. Data for 2003 only consider committees from 11 legislatures (N of total committee seats: 1394 'feminine', 1894 'masculine'). Data for 2007 consider committees from 18 legislatures (N of total committee seats: 2518 'feminine', 2451 'masculine'). The same MPs may sit in several committees.

TABLE 6
Percentage of committees with a proportion of female MPs higher than 40%

	'Traditional feminine' Committees	'Traditional masculine' Committees
2003	67.5	34.7
2007	71.0	36.2

Source: own elaboration. Data taken from legislatures' websites. Data for 2003 only consider committees from 11 legislatures (N of committees: 80 'feminine', 95 'masculine'). Data for 2007 consider committees from 18 legislatures (N of committees: 152 'feminine', 149 'masculine').

Taking the analysis further, the data permits looking into whether horizontal discrimination also affects committee leadership positions (committee presidents/chairs and committee presidency boards) before and after the quota was established. Again, these positions are decided by the parliamentary party leaders. The evidence reveals a slight increase (2.4 points) in the proportion of female committee presidents only in the traditionally 'masculine' committees. Yet there still exists a large gap of 16.4 points with women's leadership in 'feminine' committees, as shown in Table 7. Similar patterns can be observed with regard to committee presidency board membership: the gap between the two categories of committees diminished almost by half to about 12 points. Yet this was due mostly to a reduction of women in board positions in traditionally 'feminine' committees. The respective figures are, nevertheless, close to or above gender balance (defined as 40%).

These data as a whole indicate the persistence of horizontal discrimination. Nevertheless the data for each legislature reveals great variation. The number of committees with a female president has increased in many parliaments, but not in all of them, between 2003 and 2007. However, there are many legislatures in which gender balance has still not been attained among committee chairs. This is much more common among the traditionally 'masculine' committees than in the 'feminine' ones, both in 2003 and—to a lesser extent—in 2007, as Table 8 shows.

The same can be said regarding the committee presidency board positions. Horizontal discrimination was slightly reduced in most legislatures after the legal quota was passed, even if it strongly persists in most cases. Gender balance is still much more common in 'feminine' portfolio committees than in 'masculine' ones (see Table 9).

TABLE 7
Female MPs in governing committee positions

	% of female committee presidents		% of female members of Committee Presidency Boards	
	'Feminine'	'Masculine'	'Feminine'	'Masculine'
2003	52.5	33.7	58.1	37.0
2007	52.6	36.2	51.5	39.7

Source: own elaboration. Data taken from legislatures' websites. Data for 2003 only consider committees from 11 legislatures (N of committee presidents: 80 'feminine', 95 'masculine'; N of CPB positions: 260 and 327, respectively). Data for 2007 consider committees from 18 legislatures (N of committee presidents: 152 'feminine', 149 'masculine'; N of CPB positions: 485 and 496, respectively).

TABLE 8

Percentage of committees chaired by a female MP in each Spanish legislature, by committee portfolio

	'Feminine' committees		'Masculine' committees	
	2003	**2007**	**2003**	**2007**
Congreso Diputados	45.5	50.0	20.0	14.3
Andalusia	70.0	70.0	33.3	33.3
Aragon	57.1	42.9	20.0	33.3
Asturias	20.0	50.0	20.0	42.9
Balearic Islands	25.0	42.9	42.9	50.0
Canary Islands	75.0	80.0	25.0	36.4
Cantabria		50.0		16.7
Castile-La Mancha	66.7	40.0	62.5	75.0
Castile-Leon	62.5	58.3	57.1	42.9
Catalonia		64.3		22.2
Extremadura	14.3	33.3	20.0	37.5
Galicia		40.0		33.3
La Rioja	40.0	83.3	28.6	14.3
Madrid		60.0		50.0
Murcia		25.0		50.0
Navarra		66.7		30.0
Basque Country	71.4	42.9	57.1	50.0
Valencia		42.9		44.4

Source: see Table 7.

TABLE 9

Female MPs in committee presidency boards, by kind of committee (aggregated % of all the positions in each legislature)

	'Feminine' committees		'Masculine' committees	
	2003	**2007**	**2003**	**2007**
Congreso Diputados	44.9	45.2	29.9	30.4
Andalusia	55.9	54.3	42.5	43.9
Aragon	61.9	42.9	17.6	30.0
Asturias	46.7	55.6	33.3	45.5
Balearic Islands	50.0	57.1	33.3	50.0
Canary Islands	83.3	53.3	34.2	51.4
Cantabria		66.7		22.2
Castile-La Mancha	63.9	53.3	70.8	58.3
Castile-Leon	70.8	55.6	52.4	52.2
Catalonia		46.3		26.7
Extremadura	42.9	40.7	30.0	45.8
Galicia		23.5		37.9
La Rioja	40.0	72.2	33.3	38.1
Madrid		50.0		44.4
Murcia		41.7		44.4
Navarra		72.2		25.0
Basque Country	90.5	57.1	39.1	34.6
Valencia		53.3		50.0

Source: see Table 7.

Concluding Remarks

This article analyses the effectiveness of the legal quota established in Spain in 2007, comparing trends following elections in 18 parliaments before and after the quota was introduced. The aim was to gauge the impact of the quota on the election of female MPs and patterns of vertical and horizontal discrimination, in terms of access to chamber and committee leadership positions, and assignments to particular types of committees.

Using descriptive statistics mainly from two elections (those held right before and after the quota), the analysis shows that even if the quota improved the presence of female MPs (both in seats and in their share of leading positions), its impact was more limited in terms of achieving gender balance and reducing the patterns of vertical and horizontal discrimination. The increase of the numbers of women in the 18 Spanish parliaments was not as big as might have been expected with the adoption of a legal quota. The wide variations among the 18 parliaments and among the same party parliamentary groups do not point to a simple explanation.

Half of the 2007 legislature presidents were female, compared to seven out of 18 before the quota was passed. Its impact is smaller regarding to the presidency boards and even party speakers boards. On the other hand, gender balance (defined as 40%) was achieved regarding committee presidencies and committee presidency boards positions on average for the 18 legislatures, even if differences between legislatures persisted.

When comparing committee types (traditionally 'feminine' and 'masculine' portfolios), the patterns of horizontal discrimination persist after the quota, both regarding committee allocation and female share of governing positions (committee presidency and presidency boards): large gaps persist in this regard, even if there was an improvement in the proportion of women in 'masculine' committees. Again, there were remarkable differences among parliaments in this regard.

The differences among parliaments do not seem to be explained by variations in electoral results, governing party in each legislature or the existence of a prior regional gender quota. MPs' preferences for committee assignments rather appear to be reinforced by political factors within each party and in each legislature, shaping patterns in appointments for leading positions and committee allocation.

The overall conclusion of this study is that, while the quota increased the number of female MPs as well as their share of leading positions and in parliamentary committees of all types, it has not been fully effective in reducing all gender gaps—most notably, the gaps between male and female allocation and leadership of 'feminine' and 'masculine' committees. These findings support previous works that find quotas may play a crucial role in increasing the proportion of women in politics, but do not always lead necessarily to gender-balanced institutions (Krook 2009; Paxton et al. 2010). Previous literature shows, as has been done here, that there were improvements reducing vertical and horizontal discrimination in the last decades, but these patterns still persist in many countries, both in cabinets and legislatures (Dahlerup and Leyenaar 2013; Davis 2007; Escobar-Lemmon and Taylor-Robinson 2005; Krook and O'Brien 2012; Paxton et al. 2010). These patterns of discrimination reverse as more women access leading political positions (Kittilson 2006; Krook 2009), which makes it necessary to analyse other non-quota initiatives to promote gender equality (Krook and Norris 2014), as may result from applying 'quotas' to leading and governing positions within representative institutions in order to make them gender-balanced.

These findings chart a new direction in gender quota research, highlighting the need to explore whether quotas contribute to a broader transformation of access to positions of political power. Further research is needed, however, to account for the variations that exist among the legislatures analysed in this article, probing further into the role of institutional differences and political party life in the 18 legislatures, to help uncover how quotas may or may not facilitate greater gender equality in politics.

ACKNOWLEDGEMENTS

This text was presented at the ECPR Joint Sessions, Mainz, 11–15 March 2013. I want to thank all participants in the panel 'Electoral Quotas and Political Representation: Comparative Perspectives' for their valuable comments and suggestions that were very useful to improve the original text.

FUNDING

This work was supported by the Spanish National Scientific Research Plan, Grant ref. CSO2009-14381-C03-03.

NOTES

1. On international factors promoting quota diffusion, see Krook (2009) and UN (1995).
2. Balearic Islands and Castille-La Mancha in 2002 and the Basque Country and Andalusia in 2005. On the specifics of these regional quotas see Serra (2011).
3. The elections I consider are the national ones held in 2004 and 2008, as well as the regional ones held in 2003 and 2007.
4. This is the governing body of the legislature. In the national Congreso de los Diputados it has nine members. In the regional legislatures it usually has five members, but seven in Madrid and Catalonia and eight in Andalusia.
5. This is an important negotiating body within each legislature.
6. It was not possible to gather the data on the committees for seven legislatures: Cantabria, Catalonia, Galicia, Madrid, Murcia, Navarra and Valencia.
7. The budget each committee controls were disregarded because in some of them a large budget is necessarily spent paying salaries and thus is not available to develop policies (i.e., Education, Justice, Defence). National MPs were asked in semi-structured interviews conducted in 2014 to classify committee portfolios, but the results were not conclusive, apart from the 'feminine–masculine' distinction. Finally, the degree of committee prestige resulted in a classification very similar to the one using the 'masculine–feminine' distinction, with very few exceptions. For a classification of committees with these criteria, see Krook and O'Brien (2012).
8. Committees with traditionally 'feminine' portfolios are: Health, Education and Science, Women Affairs and Gender Equality, Culture and Sports, International Cooperation, Social Affairs, Immigration, Housing, Integration Policies for Handicapped People, Environment, Citizens Petitions. When a committee combined both portfolios, it was linked to the one having the heaviest weight in that particular parliament.

9.   Committees with traditionally 'masculine' portfolios are Foreign and European Union Affairs, Defence, Economy, Budget and Taxation, Public Administration, Public Works and Infrastructures, Industry, Commerce and Tourism, Justice Interior and Territorial Affairs, Labour, Agriculture and Fishing, Constitutional Affairs, Home Rules and MPs Statute. Tourism is considered a 'masculine' portfolio committee in Spain, given its weight in the gross domestic product (approximately, 11% in 2013).

References

CHILDS, SARAH and MONA L. KROOK. 2006. Should feminists give up on critical mass? A contingent yes. *Politics and Gender* 2 (4): 522–30.

CHRISTMAS-BEST, VERONA and ULRIK KJAER. 2007. Why so few and why so slow: women as parliamentary representatives in Europe from a longitudinal perspective. In *Democratic Representation in Europe: Diversity, Change and Convergence*, edited by Maurizio Cotta and Heinrich Best. Oxford: Oxford University Press, pp. 77–105.

DAHLERUP, DRUDE. 2006. *Women, Quotas and Politics.* London: Routledge.

DAHLERUP, DRUDE and MONIQUE LEYENAAR. 2013. The move towards gender balance in politics in old and new democracies. Paper presented at the 3rd European Conference on Politics and Gender, Barcelona, March.

DARCY, ROBERT. 1996. Women in the state legislative power structure: committee chairs. *Social Science Quarterly* 77 (4): 888–98.

DAVIS, REBECCA H. 2007. *Women and Power in Parliamentary Democracies. Cabinet Appointments in Western Europe, 1968–1992.* Lincoln: University of Nebraska Press.

DRUCKMAN, JAMES N. and PAUL V. WARWICK. 2005. The missing piece: measuring portfolio salience in western European parliamentary democracies. *European Journal of Political Research* 44: 17–42.

ESCOBAR-LEMMON, MARIA and MICHELLE M. TAYLOR-ROBINSON. 2005. Women ministers in Latin American government: when, where, and why? *American Journal of Political Science* 49 (4): 829–44.

FRANCESCHET, S. and PISCOPO, J. M. 2008. Gender quotas and women's substantive representation: lessons from Argentina. *Politics & Gender* 4 (3): 393–425.

HEATH, ROSEANNA M., LESLIE A. SCHWINDT-BAYER and MICHELLE M. TAYLOR-ROBINSON. 2005. Women on the sidelines: women's representation on committees in Latin American legislatures. *American Journal of Political Science* 49 (2): 420–36.

INTER-PARLIAMENTARY UNION. 2014. Women in national parliaments, archive of statistical data. Available at www.ipu.org/wmn-e/world.htm, accessed June 2014.

JONES, MARK P. 2005. The desirability of gender quotas: considering context and design. *Politics and Gender* 1 (4): 645–52.

KITTILSON, MIKI C. 2006. *Challenging Parties, Changing Parliaments: Women and Electoral Office in Contemporary Western Europe.* Columbus: Ohio State University Press.

KROOK, MONA LENA. 2009. *Quotas for Women in Politics. Gender and Candidate Selection Reform Worldwide.* Oxford: Oxford University Press.

KROOK, MONA L. and PIPPA NORRIS. 2014. Beyond quotas: strategies to promote gender equality in elected office. *Political Studies* 62 (1): 2-20.

KROOK, MONA L. and DIANA Z. O'BRIEN. 2012. All the presidents men? The appointment of female cabinet ministers worldwide. *The Journal of Politics* 74 (3): 840–55.

LAVER, MICHAEL and KENNETH A. SHEPSLE (eds). 1994. *Cabinet Ministers and Parliamentary Government.* Cambridge: Cambridge University Press.

OÑATE, PABLO. 2000. Parlamento, Grupos Parlamentarios y partidos. Los partidos políticos en el Congreso de los Diputados. In *El Congreso de los Diputados*, edited by Antonia Martínez. Madrid: Tecnos, pp. 95–140.

OÑATE, PABLO. 2008. Los partidos políticos en la España democrática. In *La España del siglo XXI*, edited by Salustiano Del Campo and José-Félix Tezanos. Madrid: Sistema, pp. 617–43.

OÑATE, PABLO. 2011. Cuotas, cantidad y calidad del incremento de la representación de las mujeres en España. In *Alcanzando el equilibrio. El acceso y la presencia de las mujeres en los parlamentos*, edited by Irene Delgado. Valencia: Tirant lo Blanch, pp. 118–35.

OÑATE, PABLO and IRENE DELGADO. 2006. Partidos, grupos parlamentarios y diputados en las asambleas autonómicas. In *Organización y funcionamiento de los parlamentos autonómicos*, edited by Pablo Oñate. Valencia: Tirant lo Blanch, pp. 135–72.

PAXTON, PAMELA, MELANIE M. HUGHES and JENNIFER L. GREEN. 2006. The international women's movement and women's political representation, 1893–2003. *American Sociological Review* 71 (6): 898–902.

PAXTON, PAMELA, MELANIE M. HUGHES and MATTHEW A. PAINTER II. 2010. Growth in women's political representation: a longitudinal exploration of democracy, electoral system and gender quotas. *European Journal of Political Research* 49 (1): 25–52.

PITKIN, HANNA. 1967. *The Concept of Representation.* Berkeley: University of California Press.

SERRA, ROSARIO. 2011. El acceso de las mujeres al Parlamento. Democracia paritaria voluntaria y exigencia legal de equilibrio de sexos. In *Alcanzando el equilibrio. El acceso y la presencia de las mujeres en los Parlamentos*, edited by Irene Delgado. Valencia: Tirant lo Blanch, pp. 41–82.

STUDLAR, DONLEY T. and GARY F. MONCRIEF. 1999. Women's work? The distribution and prestige of portfolios in the Canadian provinces. *Governance* 12 (4): 374–95.

SWERS, MICHELE L. 2002. *The Difference Women Make: The Policy Impact of Women in Politics.* Chicago: University of Chicago Press.

THRELFALL, MONICA. 2007. Explaining gender parity representation in Spain: the internal dynamics of parties. *West European Politics* 30 (5): 1068–95.

UNITED NATIONS. 1995. Beijing Declaration and Platform for Action (adopted at the 16th plenary meeting, 15 September 1995). Fourth World Conference on Women, Beijing, September. Available at http://www.un.org/womenwatch/daw/beijing/platform/, accessed March 2013.

VERGE, TANIA. 2006. Mujer y partido político en España: Las estrategias de los partidos y su impacto institucional. *Revista Española de Investigaciones Sociológicas* 115: 165–96.

ZETTERBERG, PÄR. 2008. The downside of gender quota? Institutional constraints on woman in Mexican state legislatures. *Parliamentary Affairs* 61 (3): 442–60.

TRACING GENDER DIFFERENCES IN PARLIAMENTARY DEBATES: A GROWTH CURVE ANALYSIS OF UGANDAN MPS' ACTIVITY LEVELS IN PLENARY SESSIONS, 1998–2008

Vibeke Wang

Participation in legislative debates is potentially an important tool for Members of Parliament (MPs) to communicate policy positions and exert influence on the policy process. Yet there are few studies of legislative speech behaviour, and specifically gendered analyses are sparse. This article examines how gender and gender quotas affect speech activity measured in terms of how much MPs speak on the floor of the Ugandan parliament. An original dataset constructed from transcripts of parliamentary debates spanning a ten-year period (1998–2008) is applied in the analyses. Controlling for other possible determinants of speech activity, it is found that, contrary to expectations, there are no significant differences by gender in overall speech activity, but female MPs who hold parliamentary leadership positions speak significantly more than any other group. Differences between female quota MPs and their counterparts in parliament are also ruled out, countering common expectations in the quota literature.

The recent influx of women in national legislatures in sub-Saharan Africa, mainly via gender quotas, has ensured the enhanced presence of female members of parliament (MPs). It is still unclear, however, whether women are able to translate their presence into agency in the same way as their male counterparts—and, moreover, whether there are differences between female representatives elected with and without quotas. Overall, gendered analyses of parliamentary debates are sparse and few studies have specifically explored how quotas affect legislators' behaviour (but see Chaney 2006; Franceschet and Piscopo 2008; Piscopo 2011; Xydias 2008). This article addresses this gap in the literature by examining how gender, and gender quotas, affect speech activity. How much representatives participate in debates reveals whether they are favourably positioned and willing to advance policy concerns. I explore whether female MPs elected through quotas perform on par with their non-quota colleagues, male and female, on the floor of parliament in order to have equal influence on the process of legislative decision-making.

To examine these dynamics, this article uses an original dataset constructed from plenary proceedings in the Ugandan parliament between 1998 and 2008, focusing on how much a representative speaks on the parliamentary floor. MPs' speech contributions are taken to be indicative of both potential power and influence in the policy process. So far research on the impact of gender and gender quotas have mainly been conducted within a theoretical framework based on Hanna Pitkin's (1967) concepts of representation. I argue that in order to fully capture the impact of gender and gender quotas it is also necessary to pay attention to who takes the parliamentary floor and why, yet such research is still largely missing.

Uganda is a pioneer of reserved seat policies in sub-Saharan Africa. The quota system ensures that parliament includes one female quota representative for every district. As new districts have been formed, the number of women in parliament has increased dramatically from 18% in 1996 to 35% after the 2011 general elections. Because women are also elected to open seats, this case enables a comparison of quota and gender effects in relation to speech patterns. A hierarchical growth curve analysis is used to explore determinants of MPs' speech activity, taking into account gender and mode of election.

Drawing on literature in political science and psychology, I hypothesise that female MPs will engage less in plenary debates than male MPs. Moreover, women MPs in leadership positions are expected to speak less than their male counterparts on the floor. Based on findings in the quota literature suggesting that quota recipients may be, to a larger extent than other representatives, more pliable, strongly beholden to party leaders, and relegated to subordinate or token positions (see, for example, Bauer 2008a; Goetz 2003; Gosh 2003; Meena 2004), it is hypothesised that female quota MPs will speak less than non-quota MPs on the floor of parliament.

The article finds that, contrary to expectations, there are no significant differences by gender in overall speech trajectories. Intriguingly, the effect of positional power on speech level varies with gender, with female MPs who hold parliamentary leadership positions speaking significantly more than any other group. Differences between quota and non-quota women are also ruled out, countering common expectations in the quota literature of women as a submissive and pliable 'vote bank' for the incumbent party. Women MPs are by no means invisible in decision-making, and while the possibility remains that their speech activity is 'tokenistic' in the sense of having little autonomy to speak in accordance with their own convictions, the analysis does not indicate that women are any different from their male colleagues in this respect.

Hypothesising about the Effects of Gender and Quotas on Speech Activity

Gender and Talking Time

Studies focusing on gender and legislative behaviour typically focus on voting patterns and the introduction of women-friendly policies. A small body of political science scholarship examines gender and speech contributions (Bäck et al. 2014; Kathlene 1994, 2005; Mattei 1998), but most of these studies focus on speech content. Consequently, we know little about speech quantity, or to what extent women representatives in fact participate in debates as a whole. Research in psychology supports the assumption that the speaking time for men and women may differ in debates. Research on the total amount of time spent talking in group contexts has pointed to the centrality of gender as a main factor for explaining talking time (Brescoll 2012; Mast 2002). Regardless of power differences, women tend to engage less in verbal aggressiveness or dominant behaviour. Studies of language, gender and political debates show that women do not break debate rules to gain advantage as much as their male counterparts (Christie 2003; Edelsky and Adams 1990; Shaw 2000, 2006).

Scholars point to cultural stereotypes about gender and expectations related to social roles as a reason that men and women behave differently. Assuming responsibilities at home, women develop traits that manifest communal and less aggressive behaviour (Eagly 1987; Eagly and Wood 1991). The prevailing political culture of masculinity engrained in legislative assemblies and organisations such as political parties may also act as a major obstacle to female politicians (Lovenduski 2005; see also Duerst-Lahti 2005; Whip 1991). In contrast to the above literature, Brescoll (2012) finds no main effect of gender on senators' speaking time in the United States. Taken together, this theoretical and empirical research would predict that female members of parliament are less vocal during plenary discussions than male members.

Hypothesis 1: Women representatives speak less than their male counterparts on the floor of parliament.

Interaction of Gender and Power on Talking Time

Participation in chamber debates may also be determined by positional power together with gender, such that women in leadership positions will speak less than male leaders. One key explanation is fear of backlash, which may deter women from engaging in debates in the same way as their male counterparts despite holding a leadership position. The risk of backlash may increase when women's numbers rise since male colleagues may feel threatened and close down space for women's participation and influence (Grey 2006; Heath et al. 2005; Kathlene 2005). In psychology, status incongruity theory suggests that women in positions of power can generate backlash (Rudman et al. 2012).

Men and women may also approach and use their positional power differently (Blair and Stanley 1991). Women chairing committee hearings are found to participate and interrupt less than male chairs in a study at the US state level (Kathlene 1994: 565). Another study finds a strong positive relationship between power and time spent talking on the US Senate floor for male legislators, but not for female senators (Brescoll 2012). These results comply with organisational research finding that women have a more democratic, inclusive and non-hierarchical leadership style. Conversely, men tend to adopt a more autocratic style (Eagly and Carli 2007). This suggests that male leaders, more than their female counterparts, would be willing to dominate verbally for a disproportionally longer amount of time in debates to maintain and assert their status and position in the power hierarchy (Mast 2002).

Hypothesis 2: Women in leadership positions will speak less than men holding leadership positions on the floor of parliament.

Quotas and Talking Time

Research on the impact of quotas has mainly been focused on substantive representation and the content of speech contributions, and has largely ignored legislative speech quantity. Yet from a power perspective there are also good reasons to examine legislative speech time. Some scholars propose that quotas make it more likely that women representatives advance women's concerns due to a perceived *mandate* to act for women. At the same time they suggest that quotas also reinforce *labels* in the form of negative stereotypes of women as less competent, with a negative impact on women's substantive representation (Franceschet and Piscopo 2008). The label effect implies a stigma, namely that quota representatives are less qualified and deserving of their positions than their non-quota counterparts.

This suggests that they are 'token' representatives, pliable and easily controlled by the party elites. The consequence may be that female quota recipients shy away from taking on a mandate to act on behalf of women (Childs and Krook 2012; Franceschet and Piscopo 2008). Tokenism could also lead to general inactivity, leading to fewer speech contributions on the parliament floor.

Reserved seat quotas have been considered especially prone to the above weaknesses, especially in African countries with dominant party systems in which the party and the executive influence and control the quota system (Devlin and Elgie 2008; Disney 2006; Muriaas and Wang 2012; Tripp 2006; Yoon 2011). In Uganda, studies have found that the quota policy has been used to bolster the incumbent party (Bauer 2008b; Green 2010; Muriaas and Wang 2012), in this way promoting women who are loyal to the governing party (Goetz 2003; Tripp 2006). The strong ties between the ruling party and quota representatives may further relegate the latter to take positions as subordinate or tokens (Bauer 2008a: 362, 2008b; Goetz 2003: 118).

A second criticism against quotas in general relates to MPs' qualifications and backgrounds, with quota women being assumed to lack competence—and thus being less likely to speak during plenary debates. Recent research finds that quota representatives do tend to bring different types of qualifications and experiences to office, yet they are not unprepared or unqualified (Franceschet and Piscopo 2012; Murray 2012; O'Brien 2012). Findings from Uganda show that contrary to expectations quota women are not less qualified than their non-quota counterparts (Josefsson 2014; O'Brien 2012). These findings contradict the expectation that quota women should talk less than other representatives based on merit.

Although the literature demonstrates conflicting findings, the broader debate might lead to the overall expectation that quota women should talk less in parliament than their male and female counterparts.

Hypothesis 3: Female quota recipients will speak less than non-quota mandated representatives on the floor of parliament.

The speech activity of parliamentarians in the plenary may be shaped by a number of structural and personal factors other than gender and quotas, including the balance of power between backbenchers and party leaders (Proksch and Slapin 2012). Further, MPs holding leadership positions, in their mere capacity of being leaders, could also be expected to appear more frequently on the floor and speak at greater length than rank-and-file members. Research in psychology finds, for example, that high-power individuals may simply feel entitled or required to talk more than others (Brescoll 2012; Fiske 2010). Party affiliation and party discipline could also be critical with respect to speech activity, with ruling party MPs being expected to talk less than opposition members. Finally, time served in parliament may also be an important determinant. Alternative explanations of speech activity are controlled for by including variables with information on position, party affiliation, experience, introduction of a multiparty system and background characteristics (age and regional belonging).

The Case of Uganda

Uganda can be considered as a 'most likely' case of finding gender differences in how much MPs speak in parliament. Uganda has among the highest shares of women in parliament in the world, yet it remains a strictly patriarchal society. Parliament is a deeply conservative institution and its institutional norms and internal structures and routines can be seen as inhibiting to women representatives (Tamale 1999; Tripp 2006).

The reserved seat system has also been widely criticised. The quota policy was introduced in 1989 in a top-down fashion spurred by the ruling National Resistance Movement (NRM) government's need to create regime legitimacy and stability, propelled as well in part from below by emerging trends in the international and national women's movement (Muriaas and Wang 2012). Historically, close ties between women and the NRM, together with the constraints of patronage politics, has been considered the reason behind women's relatively poor legislative record from 1996 to 2006 (Goetz 2002; Tamale 1999; Tripp 2006). This was related in particular to the use of electoral colleges to elect women district representatives prior to 2006 (Goetz 2002; Tamale 1999). Uganda thus constitutes a likely case of finding gender differences in speech activity, at the same time that its quota design enables a comparison of gendered versus quota effects.

The incumbent, President Museveni, and the NRM have currently ruled Uganda for more than 25 years. During what is known as the Movement years (1986–2006), a so-called 'no-party system' was established. Under this system, candidates were elected individually, with political parties being prohibited from participating. Partly as a result of this, political parties in Uganda are generally weak, although the dominant NRM has a more elaborate political organisation and greater capacity than the opposition parties (Kiiza et al. 2008). A multiparty system was reintroduced quite unexpectedly in 2005, yet Uganda still qualifies as hybrid regime with excessive power concentration in the executive (Tripp 2010). A simple plurality majority electoral system is utilised for the directly elected seats at the national level. Female district quota representatives in parliament are elected by universal suffrage at the district level in separate elections for women.

The Speaker or Deputy Speaker presides over parliamentary proceedings, regulates debates, and controls the speakers' list. Any MP wishing to speak must 'catch the Speaker's eye' by standing or half standing and may take the floor only if called to do so by the Speaker. Although MPs formally are free to take the floor, within the NRM in particular loyalty is rewarded and there are effective informal mechanisms of sanction such as withdrawal of party support in elections.

Plenary sessions are 'on the record' and subject to quite broad press coverage. This means that MPs may direct their speeches at different audiences. Plenary proceedings are covered by both radio and television channels. There is a press gallery in the parliamentary chamber and various modes of parliamentary outreach. All the same, there is still relatively low awareness of legislative work in Uganda (Humphreys and Weinstein 2012: 2–3).

Data, Variables and Method

The dataset applied is constructed from transcripts of parliamentary debates (the Parliamentary Hansards) spanning a ten-year period, allowing for a unique longitudinal perspective. The sample size is relatively large, including a total of 2954 observations. The dependent variable is operationalised as the total number of lines contributed by each representative in transcripts from plenary debates per year. This variable reveals how well-placed MPs are to pursue their interests and to influence the legislative process. Active debaters are in most circumstances better positioned to advance their concerns. The variable is not intended to capture what issues MPs dedicate their time to in the plenary nor does it capture the quality or substance of performance.

To evaluate the hypotheses, the model build starts with a simple unconditional linear growth model as a base. It is gradually expanded on in multiple steps by adding explanatory variables at the respective levels in a mixed effects model. The lowest level (level 1) variables are time-variant and include variables accounting for MPs' experience in parliament, mode of election, and positional power held. The highest level (level 2) variables are time-invariant. Variables falling into this category are gender, regional belonging, party membership, age, an aggregate variable for experience, and a dummy for the introduction of a multiparty system. The number of measurements is not the same for all MPs and there is also turnover among the MPs since the data cover two elections (2001 and 2006).

The subsequent analyses are run with the 'vce robust' option in Stata to correct for heteroskedasticity and ensure robust standard deviations (Wooldridge 2006). Correlation in the residual structure is expected in time-series data and an unstructured covariance matrix is therefore specified. The growth curve models are fit using maximum likelihood estimation, and the deviance statistic is used as an indication of how well the models fit the data. Standard fit indices like the Akaike's Information Criterion (AIC) and Schwarz's Bayesian Information Criterion (BIC) are also used to compare the models.

Growth curve analysis allows for causal heterogeneity and the possibility that effects may change over time. In this study each MP in the dataset has a separate growth curve. Of importance are differences across gender in verbal activity (and the development of this relationship over time), as well as intra-group disparities among women. The empirical analysis is structured according to the following logic: first the *trend* in MPs' speech is examined to establish how much the speech level of male and female MPs change over time. Second, whether there are any gendered differences and *variation* in the trend of MPs' speech is investigated. The final part of the analysis concerns what intra-individual (level 1) and inter-individual (level 2) predictors *account* for variation in how much MPs talk, with specific focus on gender-related effects.

Plenary Speech Activity in the Ugandan Parliament

Broken down according to gender, the summary statistics for the dependent variable shows that contrary to expectations, female legislators on average speak more than their male counterparts in the plenary proceedings, but the difference is modest and not significant according to a simple t-test.[1] As the maximum number of lines spoken is considerably higher for male than for female MPs, this most likely indicates that there are a few male MPs who take the floor more than anyone else.

To further investigate MPs' speech patterns, a base unconditional linear growth model for speech level is compared to a polynomial quadratic model accounting for curvilinearity, and it is found that the latter is a better fit. Results are reported in Table 1 (Models 1 and 2). The linear model indicates that MPs are getting more active as they acquire more experience and reveals considerable variation in how much MPs speak already at the beginning of the time period. The MPs have different starting points, and this in turn affects their later speech trajectories. Legislators that talk a lot at the outset increase their activity level faster than their fellow MPs. One interpretation is that personal qualities, like being an extrovert or introvert, is important. Other explanations relate to educational and previous political experience.

Having established that the shape of the growth curves are nonlinear over time and varies with experience the next step is to evaluate the hypotheses by identifying what account for how much parliamentarians speak during plenary sessions by examining predictors of change and cross-level interactions.

Table 1
Growth models for change in how much MPs speak in plenary debates (Models 1–3)

Fixed effects	Model 1 + linear/rand coef		Model 2+ quadratic		Model 3 + level 1 var	
	Coef.	SE	Coef.	SE	Coef.	SE
Level 1						
Intercept	234.71	16.47	152.62	18.11	224.37	37.55
Experience	18.05*	5.13	102.27*	10.07	101.40*	10.35
Experience²			−11.93*	1.22	−11.94*	1.24
Position					−89.78*	29.25
Mode of election					7.11	33.20
Random effects	*Variance component*	*SE*	*Variance component*	*SE*	*Variance Component*	*SE*
Intercept	242.46	16.87	231.20	16.70	230.72	17.39
Experience	63.14	4.95	62.96	4.97	63.35	5.08
Level 1 residual	408.65	6.11	402.17	6.03	407.41	6.20
Corr exper_interc	0.358		0.128	0.47	0.47	0.13
Model fit						
Deviance	199.42		93.34		9.35	
Parameters	6		7		9	
AIC	44808		44717		43303	
BIC	44844		44759		43357	

Note: *Significant at the 1% level. **Significant at the 5% level.

No systematic differences are found between female MPs and their male counterparts in terms of speaking when adding the inter-individual predictor of gender (Model 4, Table 2). This effectively counters the expectation that male MPs are more active in plenary proceedings than female MPs (Hypothesis 1). This aligns with the previously conducted t-test. There is, however, significant cross-level interaction between experience and gender indicating that time-trends in speech quantity differ across women and men (see Model 5, Table 2). As seen in Figure 1, the speech trajectory for male legislators increases at a less steep rate than for female legislators. This reflects that female MPs speak more initially and thus have steeper growth trajectories than their male counterparts.

Intriguingly, the effect of positional power on speech level also varies with gender, but not as expected according to Hypothesis 2 (see Table 2 and Figure 2). High-power women talk for a longer amount of time than any other group in parliament. Explanations such as fear of backlash therefore do not seem to hold in Uganda. The negative significance attained for the interaction between position and gender (both individually and when tested collectively) confirms that there are relevant differences and that gender has a moderating effect. Female frontbenchers have a consistently higher level of speech than male frontbenchers as well as backbenchers of both sexes. This means that a limited group of women speak a lot, while the bulk of female MPs together with male backbenchers make up the least active segment in terms of speech activity. It is to be expected that holding leadership positions results in longer speaking times (the intra-individual predictor of position is significant, see Model 3, Table 1), but the considerable disparity in speech quantity between female and male leaders is striking. Gender moderates the effect of positional power, but in seemingly different directions: for female frontbenchers the effect is positive, while the effect for female backbenchers is negative.

The results reported in Model 3 (Table 1) imply that whether one is a quota district seat representative or elected to parliament on a non-quota seat does not significantly affect

Table 2

Growth models for change in how much MPs speak in plenary debates (Models 4–5)

Fixed effects	Model 4 + level 2 variables		Model 5 + Interaction	
	Coef.	SE	Coef.	SE
Level 1				
Intercept	116.49	89.24	120.33	43.33
Experience	91.27*	10.60	87.47*	10.69
Experience^2	−9.45*	1.38	−8.06*	1.49
Position	−73.43*	29.89	−18.52	34.64
Mode of election				
Level 2				
Party m'ship	−93.72*	42.27	−21.58	48.41
Experience (agg)	2.54*	1.12	3.27*	1.06
Female	20.52	36.29	178.08*	62.03
Age	1.56	1.64		
Multipartysystem	−10.66	40.55		
Cross-level				
Exper*Gender				
Position*Gender			−209.75*	64.15
Exper*Party m'ship			−19.29**	9.71
Random effects	Variance Component	SE	Variance Component	SE
Intercept	227.92	17.43	228.55	17.30
Experience	62.10	5.07	61.65	5.03
Level 1 residual	406.51	6.19	405.77	6.17
Corr exper_interc	0.45	0.13	0.42	0.13
Model fit				
Deviance	26.02		14.54	
Parameters	13		13	
AIC	43284		43271	
BIC	43362		43348	

Note: *Significant at the 1% level. **Significant at the 5% level.

speech level in plenary proceedings, in this way disproving Hypothesis 3. Quota recipients do not speak less than men and women elected from open seats (the intra-individual predictor for mode of election is not significant). As quota MPs are female this effectively counters common arguments against gender quotas, namely that quota representatives contribute less in parliament and that a reserved seat quota may create a two-tiered system of legislators, where quota MPs take the backseat. There is no evidence of this based on these data. Within level interactions between gender and party membership were tested but did not attain significant results, adding further support to this notion. The effect of party does not operate differently for male and female MPs in parliament, indicating that there is no reason to believe that female MPs are more loyal to the party line than male MPs. While membership in the NRM is significantly and highly negatively correlated with the average number of lines spoken by MPs, a possible explanation is the formalisation of a dominant party system and the imposition of strict party discipline, particularly within the ranks of the ruling party. Perhaps related to this, the reintroduction of a multiparty system in advance of the 2006 general elections is negatively, but not significantly, associated with how much parliamentarians speak.

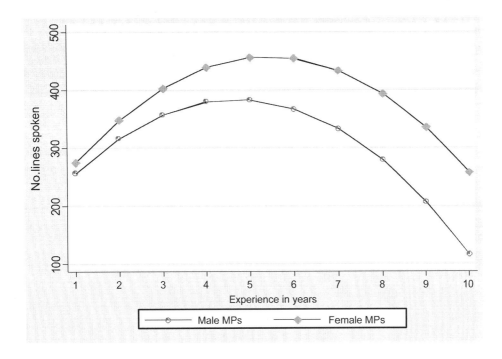

Figure 1
Predicted speech level by gender and experience.

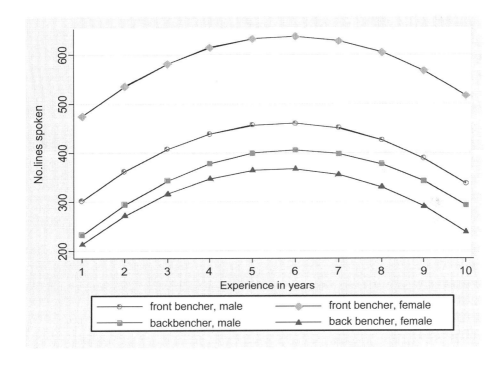

Figure 2
Predicted effects of position and gender on change in speech level.

Conclusion

This article seeks to provide insights into how gender and gender quotas affect MPs' speech behaviour during plenary sessions in the Ugandan parliament. Drawing on a diverse set of literatures focused on women's representation, as well as legislative and speech behaviour, three hypotheses about MPs' speech level in plenary proceedings are developed. The analyses are conducted using a unique dataset constructed from transcripts of plenary debates covering a ten-year period.

Uganda constitutes a 'most likely case' of finding gender differences in MPs' verbal activity, yet at first glance, the study's most interesting findings with respect to gender are in fact what it does not find. Female and male MPs do not display significantly different speech trajectories on the floor of the House, defying expectations based on social role theory. This finding could imply that over time the pervasive culture of masculinity within parliament has been transformed and become more conducive to women. This could be because gender bias in cultural practices may be challenged as more women representatives enter parliament (Chaney et al. 2007; Childs 2004b; Freedman 2002). Alternatively, women may have adapted by adopting a masculine style of politics (Childs 2004a).

Interestingly, women in leadership positions speak more than their male counterparts on the floor of parliament rather than less. Female leaders demonstrate the highest verbal activity level in parliament and have steeper growth trajectories than their male counterparts. Why women in leadership positions outperform male leaders in parliament is puzzling. Possible explanations could relate to female MPs having become more organised than male counterparts in advance of chamber sessions (Wang 2013).

Finally, in contrast to expectations put forward in the quota literature (see, for example, Bauer 2008a; Goetz 2003; Gosh 2003), mode of election to parliament does not significantly influence speech activity in parliament. Female quota recipients do not speak less than other MPs in parliament. This pattern is consistent with previous research which has found that female quota representatives in Uganda are not less qualified than their non-quota counterparts (Josefsson 2014; O'Brien 2012). Furthermore, this lack of difference between quota and non-quota MPs could indicate that the former are not more prone to manipulation and relegation to subordinate status in parliament. This notion is further supported by the fact that the effect of party on speech activity does not operate differently for male and female MPs.

Altogether, the findings show that women parliamentarians in Uganda are well-positioned to influence policy-making in parliament. They are decidedly not marginalised or 'tokens' in the sense of being invisible and passive in legislative debates. The possibility remains, however, that they are excessively loyal to the ruling party. In this respect, however, female MPs are not expected to be better or worse than their male counterparts.

The findings in this article point to a variety of new directions for future research. One would be to analyse various quantitative indicators of debate influence and acknowledged presence (see Clayton et al. 2014) (both in the plenary and parliamentary committees). Thus far, most studies of MPs' verbal behaviour have been carried out in Western Europe and North America in contexts where quotas do not exist or are voluntarily adopted by political parties. More studies are required in contexts with reserved seats in order to better understand the effects of quotas and gender on MPs' agency. Since the great majority of such quota policies have been adopted in non-Western countries, this broadens the empirical focus of the literature and may pave the way for more rigorous comparative analyses.

ACKNOWLEDGEMENTS

Comments by Mona Lena Krook, Tor Midtbø, and Pär Zetterberg greatly helped to improve earlier versions of this manuscript. The author would also like to thank participants in the ECPR Joint Session Workshop 'Electoral quotas and political representation' in Mainz, 11–16 March 2013, for valuable comments. Thanks to the Ugandan Scorecard Project for sharing data on MPs' plenary activity with me. This work was supported by the Norwegian Research Council's Effect of Aid programme and the University of Bergen.

NOTE

1.   The t-statistic is -0.8798 and the corresponding two-tailed p-value is 0.3791.

References

BÄCK, HANNA, MARC DEBUS and JOCHEN MÜLLER. 2014. Who takes the parliamentary floor? The role of gender in speech-making in the Swedish Riksdag. *Political Research Quarterly* 1–15.

BAUER, GRETCHEN. 2008a. Fifty/fifty by 2020. *International Feminist Journal of Politics* 10 (3): 348–68.

BAUER, GRETCHEN. 2008b. Uganda: reserved seats for women MPs: affirmative action for the national women's movement or the national resistance movement? In *Women and Legislative Representation*, edited by M. Tremblay. New York: Palgrave Macmillan, pp. 27–39.

BLAIR, DIANE and JEANIE R. STANLEY. 1991. Personal relationships and legislative power: male and female perceptions. *Legislative Studies Quarterly* 16 (4): 495–507.

BRESCOLL, VICTORIA. 2012. Who takes the floor and why: gender, power, and volubility in organizations. *Administrative Science Quarterly* 20 (10): 1–20.

CHANEY, PAUL. 2006. Critical mass, deliberation and the substantive representation of women. *Political Studies* 54: 691–714.

CHANEY, PAUL, FIONA MACKAY and LAURA MCALLISTER. 2007. *Women, Politics and Constitutional Change.* Cardiff: University of Wales Press.

CHILDS, SARAH. 2004a. A feminized style of politics? Women MPs in the House of Commons. *British Journal of Politics and International Relations* 6 (1): 3–19.

CHILDS, SARAH. 2004b. *New Labour's Women MPs: Women Representing Women.* London: Routledge.

CHILDS, SARAH and MONA LENA KROOK. 2012. Labels and mandates in the United Kingdom. In *The Impact of Gender Quota*, edited by Susan Franceschet, Mona Lena Krook and Jennifer M. Piscopo. New York: Oxford University Press, pp. 89–102.

CHRISTIE, CHRIS. 2003. Politeness and the linguistic construction of gender in parliament: an analysis of transgressions and apology behavior. *Sheffield Hallam Working Papers: Linguistic Politeness and Context.* Available at http://extra.shu.ac.uk/wpw/politeness/christie.htm, accessed 25 April 2013.

CLAYTON, AMANDA, CECILIA JOSEFSSON and VIBEKE WANG. 2014. Present without presence? A gendered analysis of MP debate recognition in the Ugandan parliament. *Representation*, doi: 10.1080/00344893.2014.951232.

DEVLIN, CLAIRE and ROBERT ELGIE. 2008. The effect of increased women's representation in parliament: the case of Rwanda. *Parliamentary Affairs* 61 (2): 237–54.

DISNEY, JENNIFER LEIGH. 2006. Mozambique: empowering women through family law. In *Women in African Parliaments*, edited by Gretchen Bauer and Hannah E. Britton. Boulder, CO: Lynne Rienner, pp. 31–57.

DUERST-LAHTI, GEORGIA. 2005. Institutional gendering: theoretical insights into the environment of women officeholders. In *Women and Elective Office*, edited by Sue Thomas and Clyde Wilcox. New York: Oxford University Press, pp. 230–43.

EAGLY, ALICE H. 1987. *Sex Differences in Social Behavior: A Social-Role Interpretation*. Hillsdale: Erlbaum.

EAGLY, ALICE H. and LINDA L. CARLI. 2007. *Through the Labyrinth*. Boston, MA: Harvard Business School Press.

EAGLY, ALICE H. and WENDY WOOD. 1991. Explaining sex differences in social behavior: a meta-analytic perspective. *Personality and Social Psychology Bulletin* 17: 306–15.

EDELSKY, CAROL and KAREN L. ADAMS. 1990. Creating equality: breaking the rules in debates. *Journal of Language and Social Psychology* 9 (3): 171–90.

FISKE, SUSAN. 2010. Interpersonal stratification: status, power and subordination. In *Handbook of Social Psychology*, edited by Daniel T. Gilbert and Gardner Lindzey. Hoboken, NJ: Wiley, pp. 941–82.

FRANCESCHET, SUSAN and JENNIFER M. PISCOPO. 2008. Gender quotas and women's substantive representation: lessons from Argentina. *Politics and Gender* 4 (3): 393–425.

FRANCESCHET, SUSAN and JENNIFER M. PISCOPO. 2012. Gender and political backgrounds in Argentina. In *The Impact of Gender Quotas*, edited by Susan Franceschet, Mona Lena Krook and Jennifer M. Piscopo. New York: Oxford University Press, pp. 43–56.

FREEDMAN, JANE. 2002. Women in the European parliament. *Parliamentary Affairs* 55: 179–88.

GOETZ, ANNE MARIE. 2002. No shortcuts to power: constraints on women's political effectiveness in Uganda. *Journal of Modern African Studies* 40 (4): 549–76.

GOETZ, ANNE MARIE. 2003. The problem with patronage: constraints on women's political effectiveness in Uganda. In *No Shortcuts to Power: African Women in Politics and Policy Making*, edited by Anne Marie Goetz and Shireen Hassim. New York: Zed Books, pp. 110–39.

GOSH, ARCHANA. 2003. Women's reservations and electoral politics in urban local bodies: an analysis of Chennai municipal corporation elections, 2001. *Indian Journal of Gender Studies* 10 (1): 117–41.

GREEN, ELLIOT. 2010. Patronage, district creation, and reform in Uganda. *Studies in Comparative International Development* 45 (1): 83–103.

GREY, SANDRA. 2006. Numbers and beyond: the relevance of critical mass in gender research. *Politics & Gender* 2 (4): 492–502.

HEATH, MICHELLE, ROSEANNA, LESLIE A. SCHWINDT-BAYER, AND MICHELLE M. TAYLOR-ROBINSON. 2005. Women on the sidelines: women's representation on committees in Latin American legislatures. *American Journal of Political Science* 49 (2): 420–36.

HUMPHREYS, MACARTAN and JEREMY M. WEINSTEIN. 2012. Policing politicians: citizen empowerment and political accountability in Uganda preliminary analysis. *Working Paper*, London: International Growth Centre.

JOSEFSSON, CECILIA. 2014. Who benefits from gender quotas? Assessing the impact of election procedure reform on Members of Parliament's attributes in Uganda. *International Political Science Review* 35 (1): 93–105.

KATHLENE, LYN. 1994. Power and influence in state legislative policymaking: the interaction of gender and position in committee hearing debates. *American Political Science Review* 88 (3): 560–76.

KATHLENE, LYN. 2005. In a different voice: women and the policy process. In *Women and Elective Office*, edited by Sue Thomas and Clyde Wilcox. New York: Oxford University Press, pp. 213–29.

KIIZA, JULIUS, LARS SVÅSAND and ROBERT TABARO. 2008. Organising parties for the 2006 elections. In *Electoral Democracy in Uganda*, edited by Julius Kiiza, Sabiti Makara and Lise Rakner. Kampala: Fountain Publishers, pp. 201–30.

LOVENDUSKI, JONI. 2005. *Feminizing Politics*. Cambridge: Polity Press.

MAST, MARIANNE S. 2002. Dominacne as expressed and inferred through speaking time: a meta-analysis. *Human Communication Research* 28 (3): 420–50.

MATTEI, LURA R.W. 1998. Gender and power in American legislative discourse. *Journal of Politics* 60: 440–61.

MEENA, RUTH. 2004. The politics of quotas in Tanzania. In *An Implementation of Quotas: African Experiences*, edited by Julie Ballington. International IDEA, Stockholm: Trydells Tryckeri, pp. 82–6.

MURIAAS, RARGNHILD L. and VIBEKE WANG. 2012. Executive dominance and the politics of quota representation in Uganda. *The Journal of Modern Africa Studies* 50 (2): 309–38.

MURRAY, RAINBOW. 2012. Parity and legislative competence in France. In *The Impact of Gender Quotas*, edited by Susan Franceschet, Mona Lena Krook and Jennifer M. Piscopo. New York: Oxford University Press, pp. 27–42.

O'BRIEN, DIANA Z. 2012 Quotas and qualifications in Uganda. In *The Impact of Gender Quotas*, edited by Susan Franceschet, Mona Lena Krook and Jennifer M. Piscopo. New York: Oxford University Press, pp. 57–71.

PISCOPO, JENNIFER M. 2011. Rethinking descriptive representation: rendering women in legislative debates. *Parliamentary Affairs* 64 (3): 448–72.

PITKIN, HANNA F. 1967. *The Concept of Representation*. Berkeley: University of California Press.

PROKSCH, OLIVER and JONATHAN SLAPIN. 2012. Institutional foundations of legislative speech. *American Journal of Political Science* 56 (3): 520–37.

RUDMAN, LAURIE A., CORINNE A. MOSS-RACUSIN, JULIE E. PHELAN and SANNE NAUTS. 2012. Status incongruity and backlash toward female leaders. *Journal of Experimental Social Psychology* 48: 165–79.

SHAW, SYLVIA. 2000. Language, gender and floor apportionment in political debates in the House of Commons. *Discourse and Society* 11 (3): 401–18.

SHAW, SYLVIA. 2006. Governed by the rules? The female voice in parliamentary debates. In *Speaking Out: The Female Voice in Public Contexts*, edited by Judith Baxter. New York: Palgrave Macmillan, pp. 81–102.

TAMALE, SYLVIA. 1999. *When Hens Begin to Crow: Gender and Parliamentary Politics in Uganda*. Kampala: Fountain Publishers Ltd.

TRIPP, AILI MARI. 2006. Uganda: agents of change for women's advancement? In *Women in African Parliaments*, edited by Hannah Britton and Gretchen Bauer. Boulder: Lynne Rienner, pp. 111–32.

TRIPP, AILI MARI. 2010. *Museveni's Uganda*. Boulder: Lynne Rienner.

WANG, VIBEKE. 2013. Women changing policy outcomes: learning from pro-women legislation in the Ugandan parliament. *Women's Studies International Forum* 41: 113–21.

WHIP, ROSEMARY. 1991. Representing women: Australian female parliamentarians on the horns of a dilemma. *Women and Politics* 11 (3): 1–22.

WOOLDRIDGE, JEFFREY. 2006. *Introductory Econometrics*. Mason: Lachina Publishing Services.

XYDIAS, CHRISTINA. 2008. Inviting more women to the party. *International Journal of Sociology* 37 (4): 52–66.

YOON, MI YOUNG. 2011. More women in the Tanzanian legislature: do numbers matter? *Journal of Contemporary African Studies* 29 (1): 83–98.

PRESENT WITHOUT PRESENCE? GENDER, QUOTAS AND DEBATE RECOGNITION IN THE UGANDAN PARLIAMENT

Amanda Clayton, Cecilia Josefsson and Vibeke Wang

This article charts a new direction in gender quota research by examining whether female legislators in general, and quota recipients in particular, are accorded respect and authority in plenary debates. We measure this recognition in relation to the number of times an individual member of parliament (MP) is referred to by name in plenary debates. We use a unique dataset from the Ugandan parliament to assess the determinants of MP name recognition in plenary debates over an eight-year period (2001–08). Controlling for other possible determinants of MP recognition, we find that women elected to reserved seats are significantly less recognised in plenary debates over time as compared to their male and female colleagues in open seats.

Introduction

Countries in East Africa have been at the forefront of increasing the number of women in legislatures through the use of gender quotas. Today, Rwanda has the highest proportion of women in parliament worldwide and countries such as Uganda, Tanzania and Burundi all have over 30% women in their respective parliaments (IPU 2014). Yet, the ability of quotas to increase women's physical presence in legislative bodies does not guarantee that quota recipients will have the same ability as their non-quota colleagues to shape these bodies' decisions. To do this, we argue, quota recipients' presence must generate the same respect and authority as their equivalently placed colleagues in open seats.

In this article, we explore the effects of gender and gender quotas on Ugandan legislators' plenary recognition, measured as the number of times an individual member of parliament (MP) is referred to by name in plenary debates. As we expand further below, we interpret name recognition to signal both the respect (as opposed to discrimination) an MP receives by her colleagues in parliament as well as her potential power or authority in the domain of policymaking. This study thus expands research on women's physical presence in legislatures, their descriptive representation, by examining how other MPs recognise this presence. Contributing further to the quota literature, we further analyse whether different patterns of recognition exist among women elected via quotas versus those elected in open counties.

We use a unique content analysis dataset from the Ugandan Parliamentary Hansard and find that, controlling for other possible determinants of plenary recognition including incumbency, party affiliation and total debate contributions, women who are elected to reserved seats are still significantly less recognised in plenary debates over time as compared to their male and female colleagues in open seats. Further, this trend only becomes pronounced after Uganda transitioned to multi-party rule in 2006. Highly recognised quota-mandated women from the ruling party were not reelected and the few who were reelected significantly altered their behaviour in such a way that diminished their presence and authority during plenary debates. These findings lead us to conclude that opening the democratic space in Uganda counter-intuitively had negative short-term effects on quota-mandated women's legislative recognition.

The first section reviews the literature on women's descriptive and substantive representation and situates our contribution to this field. We then introduce the Ugandan case, highlighting how certain features of the political system enable us to measure both individual- and institutional-level factors that may determine the extent to which MPs' physical presence is informally acknowledged and recognised in legislative debates. The following section introduces our dataset and methodological approach. We next present our results and offer a discussion of our findings, informed by over 100 interviews conducted between 2009 and 2013, concluding with how our findings relate to current gender quota scholarship.

Gender, Quotas and Legislative Recognition

Research on women's political representation largely takes its point of departure from Hanna Pitkin's (1967) concepts of descriptive ('standing for'), substantive ('acting for') and symbolic ('role modeling') representation. We situate our study within the frame of women's descriptive representation, but our analysis moves beyond mere presence by focusing on female legislator's recognition in the plenary as an indication of their standing within the legislature, and by extension their possibility to advance legislation on a variety of issues. Given that both quota-elected and non-quota-elected women hold seats in the Ugandan parliament, this study is also able to distinguish between the effects of gender and electoral rules on MPs' recognition in plenary debates.

While there is extensive research in terms of the impact of quotas on women's descriptive representation, only recently have scholars begun to examine characteristics of quota recipients beyond their numbers in political decision-making bodies. These studies compare quota recipients to other MPs in terms of their qualifications, loyalty and legislative independence, and ability to influence gender-related legislation.

The existing research on quota recipients' qualifications reveals no clear trend. Several studies report that in some cases quota representatives are less qualified than other representatives in terms of seniority in age (Britton 2005) and political experience (Franceschet and Piscopo 2012; Rai et al. 2006; Sater 2007) but not necessarily education (Franceschet and Piscopo 2012; Sater 2007). In a case study of Tanzania, Yoon (2011) refers to limitations due to lack of skills among female MPs. Studies of women in the Ugandan parliament, however, convincingly conclude that contrary to expectations female quota recipients are not significantly different from other representatives in terms of their relevant qualifications and skill sets (Josefsson 2014; O'Brien 2012).

Several scholars find that female quota representatives often are members of the social and economic elite and therefore easily drawn into patronage politics (Nanivedekar 2006; Rai et al. 2006; Vincent 2004). Other studies do not find that quota representatives are more likely to be elected due to favouritism and family ties than other representatives (Franceschet and Piscopo 2008; Zetterberg 2008). Reserved seats in particular have been criticised for reinforcing patronage politics, being used to bolster the incumbent party (Bauer 2008b; Matland 2006; Muriaas and Wang 2012) and thus promote women who are overly loyal to the ruling party (Goetz 2003; Tamale 1999; Tripp 2006). This can negatively affect quota recipients' ability to advance gender-related legislation, in particular when it conflicts with party interests (Tripp 2006; cf. Longman 2006; Yoon 2011).

Work has also addressed the status and possibilities for quota recipients to act for women in the parliament. Writing on Argentina, Franceschet and Piscopo (2008) demonstrate how quotas have affected women's substantive representation in contradictory ways: positively by giving them a mandate to change policy, but negatively by creating the notion that women are in need of special treatment. Zetterberg (2008), on the other hand, finds that quota women in Mexican state legislatures are no more likely than non-quota women to be marginalised and invisibilised in their legislative work.

In the East African context, dominant party systems and the workings of the ruling party have been identified as constraints on women's substantive representation. Research has stressed the intrinsic problems posed particularly by reserved seat quota systems, and how quota representatives may be relegated to subordinate or 'token' positions (Bauer 2008a: 362, 2008b; Goetz 2003: 118).

It is clear from existing research, therefore, that women's presence and stature in legislative bodies by no means guarantee an increase in women's substantive representation. To better understand the theoretical connection between 'standing for' and 'acting for', we argue here that women's recognition in plenary debates is a necessary yet not sufficient precondition for women's legislative influence in general and women's substantive representation in particular.

Gender Quotas in Uganda

Uganda became one of the first African countries to adopt a reserved seat quota in 1989. MPs in open seats are elected through a first-past-the-post system in single member constituencies, called counties, while the female legislators in reserved seats are elected in larger constituencies, called districts, covering one or several of the smaller counties. Since 1989, the number of reserved seats for women has increased in every electoral cycle as new districts have been created.[1] As of 2014, 30% of parliamentary seats were reserved for women, in addition to which women held 5% of seats in open counties. Despite this impressive proportion of female legislators, it has been suggested that the legislative influence and authority of quota recipients may be circumscribed as the ruling party has become increasingly authoritarian.

Uganda provides an interesting case for examining dynamics of recognition within parliamentary debates. First, the existence of reserved seats, as well as women elected to open seats, provides an opportunity to separate the effect of gender from that of gender quotas on patterns of legislative recognition. Second, the Ugandan system of reserved seats was introduced in 1989, enabling us to study the quota's impact over a longer duration than more recent adopters.

Plenary Recognition in the Ugandan Parliament

In this study, we measure *recognition* in terms of the number of times an individual MP is recognised by name in plenary debates. This concept thus goes beyond mere descriptive representation by examining individual MPs' actual acknowledged presence—that is, whether his or her colleagues take notice of what he or she says in a meaningful way.

In the Ugandan parliament, individual legislators are generally free to speak in the plenary whenever they want to by indicating to the Speaker that they would like to be called upon. It is only in a small number of high-profile debates where the political parties draw up lists of speakers beforehand. An individual MP's name can be mentioned in the debate for several reasons: to refer to the MP's earlier intervention, to call on the MP by name, or to reference the MP's prior statements, actions or accomplishments. As an illustration, consider the following examples from a 2004 debate.

> Thank you, **hon. Lukyamuzi** for giving way. **Hon. Ken Lukyamuzi** has been stressing a point concerning negotiations and talking peace and he is saying negotiations must take place outside Uganda. (Ms Ruth Nankabirwa, woman representative of Kiboga district)

> In conclusion, and this is in answer to **hon. Oulanyah,** my endeavour to cause dialogue does not mean that I support Kony. I am strongly opposed to Kony's activities. (Mr John Ken Lukyamuzi, county representative of Lubaga South)[2]

In order for an MP to be referred to by name, it is first necessary that the others know that MP by name, which may be difficult in a parliament of 375 members. Consequently, we interpret name recognition as showing some degree of respect to the named MP. This indicator also captures the authority and ability the named MP has to spur subsequent debate. For these reasons, we argue that degree of recognition reveals both an individual member's standing and his/her potency in the legislature

Specifically, we propose several hypotheses. First, it is possible that *all women will be equally recognised in plenary debates as compared to their male colleagues*. Because there are no significant differences between the backgrounds and qualifications among men, quota women and non-quota women in the Ugandan parliament (Josefsson 2014; O'Brien 2012), we could anticipate that these three groups act in similar ways in the plenary, leading to similar scores on plenary recognition.

Second, given that we could expect women to come in with new and sometimes contentious legislative agendas, including progressive gender-related laws (Wang 2013), it is possible that women (quota-mandated or not) will make noteworthy impacts in plenary debates causing a greater degree of recognition. Together with support from civil society to train female legislators in debate techniques, this may imply that *female MPs will have higher scores on plenary recognition compared to their male colleagues*.

Third, however, there are also reasons to expect that *women elected to reserved seats will be less recognised than their male colleagues*. A general critique against quotas is that they risk creating negative stereotypes (Franceschet and Piscopo 2008). Even though women elected through these measures may be equally qualified, they risk being perceived as second-class parliamentarians by their colleagues, as less experienced and less capable. Further, if women in reserved seats are more loyal to the ruling party than male MPs—a dynamic that some observers suggest may have grown more powerful after the move to multi-party elections—we could expect these women to raise less contentious issues (and speak less in general) and therefore be less influential and recognised during debates. In such a scenario, quota women will be marginalised or made invisible in parliamentary work, and thus simply not listened to and acknowledged in plenary debates.

Finally, given that the Ugandan parliament is a deeply gendered institution characterised by patriarchal norms, *all female legislators may struggle to receive recognition for their contributions*.

Apart from gender and seat type, several other factors may potentially affect legislators' acknowledged presence. We expect incumbents and frontbenchers to be referred to more often, even when controlling for their total debate contributions. For more anonymous MPs, such as backbenchers and legislators who are serving their first term in office, it may be more difficult to make a personal mark on the debate.

Measures and Methods

Data

Our quantitative data is coded from the Ugandan Hansard records from 2001 to 2008. The data covers records from the complete 7th Parliament (2001–06) and the beginning of the 8th Parliament (2006–11), with over 1800 observations in the unit of MP-years. Our measure of MP recognition is coded simply as the number of times that an MP is referred to by name by other MPs in the plenary. Table 1 displays the summary statistics (pooled across years) of our measure of MP recognition by our three MP seat types of interest: male MPs elected to constituency seats, female MPs elected to constituency seats, and female MPs elected to reserved seats.[3]

A series of t-tests comparing the means between these various MP groups reveals that the difference between the recognition of male MPs in constituency seats and female MPs in reserved seats is statistically significant (Welch Two Sample t-test p-value = 0.05). The differences between the other two groupings (male vs. female constituency seats and between both types of female MPs) are not statistically significant (p-values = 0.38 and 0.55 respectively). Of course, the limited number of women in constituency seats limits the likelihood that observational differences between groups will attain statistical significance.

More revealing than pooled statistics, Figure 1 plots the trend of MP recognition by seat type over time. Several trends immediately stand out. First, the number of MP references appears to be cyclical, peaking in the middle of the parliamentary term, likely as a function of the total debate activity that also peaks in this way. Second, the two types of women MPs (women in open seats and women in reserved seats) have greater variation in their influence with higher peaks and lower troughs, as compared to male MPs. Third and perhaps most strikingly, 2006 stands out as turning point after which women's name recognition and reference in parliament steeply declines. As previously noted, this year is important in the history of Ugandan parliamentary politics as the country rather unexpectedly turned from one-party (National Resistance Movement, or NRM) rule to a multi-party system.

TABLE 1
Summary statistics for MP recognition, pooled across years

	Minimum	Maximum	Mean	Standard Dev.	N
Male MPs Constituency Seats	0	224	10.53	19.92	1267
Female MPs Constituency Seats	0	54	9.13	12.23	67
Female MPs Reserved Seats	0	259	8.01	20.03	317

Note: Here we exclude other special seats (army, youth, people with disabilities, and ex-officio officers).

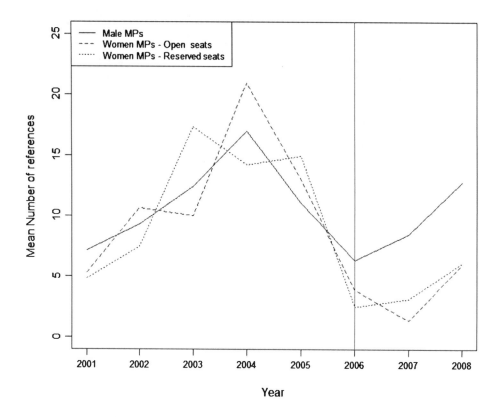

FIGURE 1
MP plenary recognition by year and seat type

Modelling MP Recognition

Moving beyond descriptive statistics, we model possible determinants of MP recognition over time. Our dependent variable, count data that is over-dispersed such that its variance is greater than its mean, follows a negative binomial distribution (see Cameron and Trivedi 1998). We model MP recognition over time as a function of various MP-level attributes and external-level variables. Our key covariate, gender/seat type, is a multinomial variable and in the models that follow, we use male MPs in constituency seats as the reference category. Our model specifications include additional covariates to account for other possible explanations of MP recognition. Specifically, we control for MP incumbency status, ruling party membership, the MP's date of birth, whether the MP is a backbencher, and the total number of lines the MP contributed to the Hansard that year. We also include individual years as fixed effects and the parliamentary term as external-level variables. Our second model specification adds interaction terms to the baseline model to measure interactions between seat type and parliamentary term as well as between seat type and NRM party membership.

Results

Table 2 shows the results of our baseline model as well as the second specification with a series of interaction terms. In our first model, with the reference category of male parliamentarians, women in reserved seats are associated with significantly fewer name

Table 2
Negative binomial regression results. Dependent variable: number of references by name

	Model 1	Model 2
Incumbent	0.468 ***	0.454 ***
	(0.061)	(0.061)
NRM	−0.245 ***	−0.197 **
	(0.091)	(0.100)
Date of Birth	0.007 **	0.007 **
	(0.003)	(0.003)
Constituency Seat Women	−0.121	19.717
	(0.144)	(136.615)
Other Representative	−0.322 ***	−0.325 ***
	(0.101)	(0.101)
Women's Representative	−0.216 ***	190.140 ***
	(0.076)	(68.944)
Year	0.090 ***	0.106 ***
	(0.023)	(0.024)
Backbencher	−0.068	−0.066
	(0.067)	(0.067)
No. of Contributions	0.025 ***	0.025 ***
	(0.001)	(0.001)
8th Parliament	−0.833 ***	−0.821 ***
	(0.115)	(0.115)
Const. Seat Women * Year		−0.010
		(0.068)
Women's Rep * Year		-0.095 ***
		(0.034)
Const. Seat Women * NRM		0.448
		(0.582)
Women's Rep * NRM		−0.369
		(0.244)
Constant	−193.259 ***	−223.063 ***
	(45.890)	(47.496)
Observations	1,820	1,820
Log Likelihood	−5,255.102	−5,250.908
Theta	0.877 ***	0.877 ***
	(0.035)	(0.035)
Akaike Inf. Crit (AIC)	10,532.200	10,531.820

Note: $^{*}p < 0.1$; $^{**}p < 0.05$; $^{***}p < 0.01$

references in the Hansard. This association, however, does not hold when comparing women in open seats to their male colleagues. Unsurprisingly, incumbents are associated with a greater number of references and MPs that speak more in general are referred to by name more often. Year fixed effects (not included in the regression table) confirm the descriptive picture in Figure 1 pertaining to the cyclical nature of this measure. We also find that NRM membership is significantly associated with less name recognition—a variable that only applies after MPs could officially identify with political parties after the move to multi-partyism in 2006. Intuitively this makes sense. Because there are fewer opposition MPs, they tend to stand out in parliamentary debates and tend to make more controversial statements.

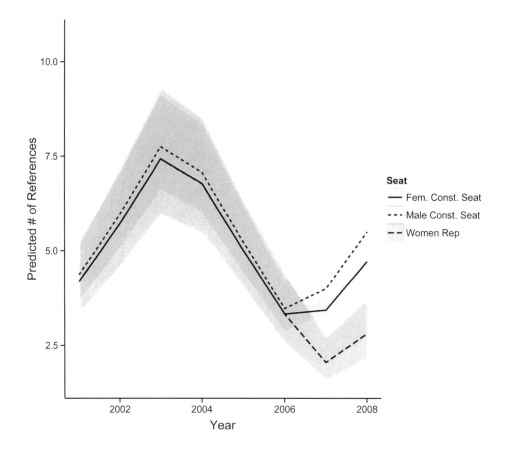

FIGURE 2
Expected values of mean references by year and seat type.

In the second model with interaction terms, we see a negative and significant interaction associated with women in reserved seats in the 8th Parliament, again confirming the descriptive trends in Figure 1. Interestingly, we also find that NRM women in reserved seats are associated with significantly fewer references by name. This pattern provides suggestive evidence in line with the notion that NRM women became more disciplined and less outspoken after the move to the multi-party system.

Regarding the magnitude of these coefficients, we simulate predicted values for our three different subgroups of interest, while holding all other values at their appropriate central tendencies. Our model results confirm our descriptive intuitions. Figure 2 plots the expected values of mean references by year with respective confidence intervals for each subgroup.

Overall the results from our statistical models are in line with our descriptive findings. The three groups are not statistically differentiable during the 7th Parliament. Within the first two years of the 8th Parliament, however, we see a clear pattern emerge in which women in reserved seats are referred to by name significantly less frequently than men in constituency seats. Whereas in 2003, two years after the beginning of the 7th Parliament, women in reserved seats were referred to by name 96% as frequently as male MPs in constituency seats (7.43 versus 7.75 times), by 2008, two years after the beginning of the 8th Parliament, women were referred to only half as frequently (51%) as their male colleagues (2.81 versus

TABLE 3
Incumbency rates for different subgroups

	Incumbency: subset of obs. 2 standard deviations above the mean (b/n 7th and 8th Parl.)	Incumbency: subset of obs. 1 standard deviation above the mean (b/n 7th and 8th Parl.)	Overall group incumbency (b/ n 7th and 8th Parl.)*	Overall group incumbency (b/ n 6th and 7th Parl.)*	% NRM among subset of obs. > 1 sd. dev. above the mean
Male MPs— Constituency Seats	40.9% (9/22)	60% (9/15)	42.1%	47.2%	88.9% (16/18)
Female MPs— Constituency Seats	50% (1/2)	0% (0/1)	66.7%	31.6%	0% (0/3)
Female MPs —Reserved Seats	25% (1/4)	50% (1/2)	33.9%	38%	0% (0/6)

Source: data from Josefsson (2014).

5.50 times). Women in constituency seats have name recognition between the other two groups during the 8th Parliament, although they are not statistically differentiable from either group, in part stemming from the limited number of observations.

Discussion

Relating to our hypotheses, we find evidence that initially all three types of MPs have similar levels of recognition during the 7th Parliament, which we would expect given their similar qualifications and backgrounds. However, this trend changes dramatically after 2006 with the election to the 8th Parliament, at which point women, particularly those elected to reserved seats, are referred to significantly less frequently than their colleagues in open seats.

Why do women lose recognition so dramatically in the 8th Parliament? Three possibilities emerge: (1) The women representatives that received the most name recognition in the 7th Parliament were not reelected to the 8th Parliament; (2) Women representatives behaved differently between the 7th and 8th Parliaments, leading to less recognition; (3) or, MPs in the 8th Parliament began to refer to women less often despite women exhibiting the same behaviour in the plenary. Further evidence suggests that our findings most likely stem from a combination of the first two scenarios.

Female MPs with High Recognition Scores Were Not Reelected

To gain leverage on which of the three explanations holds the most weight, we compare the incumbency rates of the three subsets of MPs, as well as note the party affiliation of MPs with high levels of recognition who were reelected to the 8th Parliament. Table 3 displays these descriptive statistics. We see that four women in the 7th Parliament were referred to by name over two standard deviations above the mean (over 63 times for at least one of the years of their term): Alice Alaso, Bernadette Bigirwa, Miria Matembe and Margaret Zziwa. None of these women except for Alice Alaso (an opposition member) were reelected to the 8th Parliament. Two additional women were referred to by name only one standard deviation above the mean (over 38 times for at least one year in the parliamentary term): Betty Amongi and Beatrice Kiraso. Kiraso (NRM) was not reelected to the 8th Parliament. Amongi (opposition) was reelected and continues to be referred to by name a great deal in the 8th Parliament. In sum, none of the most recognised NRM women in reserved seats in the 7th Parliament were reelected to the 8th Parliament. In contrast, close to 90% of highly recognised men reelected to the 8th Parliament were members of the NRM.

Interestingly, although much fewer in number, this pattern extends to women elected to open seats as well. In this group, there were two women who were referred to more than two standard deviations above the mean (over 41 times per year for at least one year during this term): Cecilia Atim Ogwal and Dora Byamukama. Ogwal, an opposition member, was reelected to the 8th Parliament, where she continued to be recognised at similar levels.[4] Byamukama, an NRM member, was not reelected.

The political future of virtually all ruling-party MPs, irrespective of gender, is dependent on funding from the NRM machine. MPs that do not toe the party line can be threatened with a loss of campaign funds, making their reelection chances slim.[5] According to the Ugandan scholar and woman's rights activist, Sylvia Tamale, who has followed the developments in parliament closely, 'All the outspoken women were weeded out'.[6] Moreover, openly opposing NRM leadership may lead to both physical and emotional violence. This was, for instance, the case in the lead-up to the 2001 elections, where vocal critics of Museveni were targets of such abuse (Tripp 2006: 129).

Female MPs Changed Their Behaviour

A second explanation is that female MPs might have altered their behaviour due to enhanced party discipline imposed in the 8th Parliament, or in other ways that generated less name recognition. The multi-party system has put greater pressure on MPs to toe the party line, especially within the NRM, and we have argued that this is especially salient among quota-elected women in the 8th Parliament. Further, after the transition to multi-party-ism female MPs from the NRM became more reluctant to go against the party's position.

As the then-Deputy Speaker of Parliament, an ardent supporter of women's rights issues, told us: '[before the multi-party system] people were free to speak. Today, they rather keep quiet. Some women are afraid that they speak against the party line . . . this is a hindrance to women's participation.'[7] Other respondents we interviewed confirmed this narrative. For instance, one female NRM MP explained to us: 'if you are against the party position then you are seen as an undisciplined member . . . you discuss with caution which doesn't give a free expression of views.'[8]

To test whether the general trend after 2006 is purely a function of highly recognised women leaving, our first explanation, or whether the pattern still holds among less recognised women, we remove the most recognised MPs from our observations, those that are referred to above one standard deviation from the mean for each of their respective groups. Our main results (not included here) hold when removing close to 300 of the most recognised MPs, although the magnitude of the interaction term of women's representatives in the 8th Parliament is somewhat mitigated. We interpret this to mean that our results are being driven both by the most recognised NRM women not returning to the 8th Parliament, as well as a more general trend among quota women to curtail their speech in the plenary.

The change in behaviour we witness in the 8th Parliament may also be related to a further puzzle. As Wang (2013) extensively details, despite less acknowledged presence, female MPs were successful in passing several pieces progressive gender-related pieces of legislation in the 8th Parliament. During this time, equality-promoting legislation was enacted concerning female genital mutilation (2009), prevention of trafficking in persons (2009), the establishment of an equal opportunities commission (2006), and perhaps most notably the Domestic Violence Act of 2010, the major achievement to date in family law reform in Uganda.

These accomplishments were achieved in part through an explicit strategy developed by the cross-party Uganda Women's Parliamentary Association (UWOPA). This involved breaking large pieces of progressive legislation into smaller piecemeal parts that were often less controversial, as well as active recruitment by female MPs of male MPs under the auspices of UWOPA to publicly support and even table pro-women bills. For instance, during the 8th Parliament a male UWOPA associate with a background in medicine successfully put forth a private member bill on the prohibition of female genital mutilation. The chair of UWOPA explained this strategy as follow: 'because he brought the male face on the bill it mattered, and other male MPs followed because a man is talking . . . and he is a male doctor, and he is telling us facts on this issue.'[9] Getting male MPs to advance pro-women issues could in theory contribute to less female name recognition, as the male MPs spearheading the bill receive credit in debates at the cost of female MPs that otherwise would have tabled the bills. Thus, the conscious strategy on the part of women in the 8th Parliament to focus on issues that are relatively non-divisive, as well as recruiting male sponsors, could possibly explain some of the change in recognition of female MPs. Yet is unlikely to account for the entire decline observed.

Female MPs Referred to Less Despite Similar Behaviour

A third explanation proposes that, at least to some extent, women's parliamentary standing in general may have decreased, because the most respected and high profile female legislators were no longer present in the 8th Parliament, leading to women in general becoming less recognised. These trends may have led to a general devaluation and less recognition of female parliamentarians. However, our interview data suggests otherwise. For instance, a prominent women's rights activist explicitly referred to the overall pro-equality gains made post-2006 by noting: 'I think we would need to ask silence [by women] in what regard? It's in the multiparty parliament that we got all these laws.'[10] A female legislator, when reflecting on the different parliamentary periods, referred to the 6th and 7th Parliaments as 'mainly a period of pro-women advocacy' and 'really strong voices on issues of gender . . . Now [in the 8th Parliament] I think there's more action than talk'.[11] Further, our interview data point to enhanced working relations between female and male MPs in order to realise legislative objectives.[12] Therefore, based on the narrative that emerged from extensive interviews we conclude that this explanation is the least plausible of the three.

Conclusion

Our analysis suggests that women elected through quotas do not necessarily have equal influence as their male colleagues to shape legislative outcomes. This is a crucial finding for gauging the broader meaning and impact of quotas, at a moment when countries elsewhere in Africa and around the world are adopting gender quotas. In employing a new indicator for determining individual legislators' standing and potency in the legislature, this study also contributes to the gender and politics literature by expanding research on women's numerical representation to examine the effect of gender and gender quotas on MPs' recognised presence in plenary debates. We argue that recognition in plenary debates, together with other indicators of legislators' presence and recognition, are crucial in order to better understand complex power relations within legislatures. Dynamics of recognition, we suggest, will mediate the success or failure of quota reforms to affect broader legislative agendas, and thus women's substantive representation, in the long run.

Our contribution extends the line of inquiry in the growing body of work that systematically examines MP dynamics within parliaments in at least two ways. First, our work seeks to more specifically theorise about the nexuses that emerge between the classical conceptualisations of descriptive and substantive representation. Second, our study slightly shifts the focus of analysis from what women do in parliament to how others receive them. Conceptualising female legislators' presence as recognition provides a new direction for future research. Research could further explore other measures of performance that might indicate how women elected via quotas may differ from policymakers elected through non-gender-specific rules—and what implications such measures of power dynamics have for the ways quota-elected women are able to serve their roles as representatives.

ACKNOWLEDGEMENTS

Perhaps most importantly, we are grateful to Pär Zetterberg and Mona Lena Krook for introducing us at the 2013 ECPR Joint Sessions in Mainz, for encouraging our collaboration, and for their excellent feedback on this project. We also want to gratefully acknowledge Gunnar Grendstad, Ragnhild Muriaas, Peter May and Margaret Levi who assisted or supported our cross-national collaboration. Finally, we are thankful for the feedback we received from the Midwestern Political Science Association Annual Meeting and the Western Political Science Association Annual Meeting, most notably from Amy C. Alexander and Season Hoard. Vibeke Wang acknowledges the financial support of the Norwegian Research Council's Effect of Aid programme.

NOTES

1. Women in reserved seats were first elected by an electoral college at the district level, but since 2006 they have been elected through universal adult suffrage in their respective districts.
2. Examples taken from a plenary debate on 24 June 2004 concerning the first reading of the International Criminal Court Bill.
3. Even though there are fewer women than men in the Ugandan parliament, this does not affect the individual-level mean of each of these three subgroups.
4. Ogwal moved from an open seat to a reserved seat between the 7th and 8th Parliaments.
5. This is what happened to Miria Matembe, Winnie Byanyima, Dora Byamukama and several others.
6. Sylvia Tamale, interviewed by Vibeke Wang, 2010.
7. Rebecca Kadaga interviewed by Cecilia Josefsson, January 2010.
8. Rosemary Nansubuga Seninde, interviewed by Vibeke Wang, 2010.
9. Jane Alisemera interviewed by Vibeke Wang, March 2010.
10. Jaqueline Asiimwe Mwesige, interviewed by Vibeke Wang, March 2010.
11. Beatrice Amongi Lagada, interviewed by Vibeke Wang, April 2010.
12. Ibi Florence Ekwau, interviewed by Vibeke Wang, March 2010, Rebecca Lukwago, interviewed by Vibeke Wang, April 2010, Jane Alisemera interviewed by Vibeke Wang, March 2010, and Washington Anokbonggo, interviewed by Vibeke Wang, April 2010.

REFERENCES

BAUER, GRETCHEN. 2008a. Fifty/fifty by 2020. *International Feminist Journal of Politics* 10 (3): 348–68.

BAUER, GRETCHEN. 2008b. Uganda: reserved seats for women MPs: affirmative action for the national women's movement or the national resistance movement? In *Women and Legislative Representation: Electoral Systems, Political Parties, and Sex Quotas*, edited by M. Tremblay. New York: Palgrave Macmillan, pp. 27–39.

BRITTON, HANNAH E. 2005. *Women in the South African Parliament: From Resistance to Governance.* Champaign: University of Illinois Press.

CAMERON, A. COLIN and PRAVIN K. TRIVEDI. 1998. *Regression Analysis and Count Data.* Cambridge: Cambridge University Press.

FRANCESCHET, SUSAN and JENNIFER M. PISCOPO. 2008. Gender quotas and women's substantive representation: lessons from Argentina. *Politics and Gender* 4 (3): 393–425.

FRANCESCHET, SUSAN and JENNIFER M. PISCOPO. 2012. Gender and political backgrounds in Argentina. In *The Impact of Gender Quotas*, edited by Susan Franceschet, Mona Lena Krook and Jennifer M. Piscopo. New York: Oxford University Press, pp. 43–56.

GOETZ, ANNE MARIE. 2003. The problem with patronage: constraints on women's political effectiveness in Uganda. In *No Shortcuts to Power: African Women in Politics and Policy Making*, edited by Anne Marie Goetz and Shireen Hassim. New York: Zed Books, pp. 110–139.

IPU. 2014. Women in national parliaments. Available at: http://www.ipu.org/wmn-e/classif.htm, accessed 22 March 2014.

JOSEFSSON, CECILIA. 2014. Who benefits from gender quotas? Assessing the impact of election procedure reform on Members of Parliament's attributes in Uganda. *International Political Science Review* 35 (1): 93–105.

LONGMAN, TIMOTHY. 2006. Rwanda: achieving equality or serving an authoritarian state? In *Women in African Parliaments*, edited by Gretchen Bauer and Hannah E. Britton. London: Lynne Rienner, pp. 133–50.

MATLAND, RICHARD. 2006. Electoral quotas: frequency and effectiveness. In *Women, Quotas and Politics*, edited by Drude Dahlerup. London: Routledge, pp. 275–92.

MURIAAS, RARGNHILD L. and VIBEKE WANG. 2012. Executive dominance and the politics of quota representation in Uganda. *The Journal of Modern Africa Studies* 50 (2): 309–38.

NANIVEDEKAR, MEDHA. 2006. Are quotas a good idea? The Indian experience with reserved seats for women. *Politics and Gender* 2 (1): 119–28.

O'BRIEN, DIANA Z. 2012. Quotas and qualifications in Uganda. In *The Impact of Gender Quotas*, edited by Susan Franceschet, Mona Lena Krook and Jennifer M. Piscopo. New York: Oxford University Press, pp. 57–71.

PITKIN, HANNA F. 1967. *The Concept of Representation.* Berkeley: University of California Press.

RAI, SHIRIN M., FARZANA BARI, NAZMUNNESSA MAHTAB and BIDYUT MOHANTY. 2006. South Asia: gender quotas and the politics of empowerment – a comparative study. In *Women, Quotas and Politics*, edited by Drude Dahlerup. London and New York: Routledge, pp. 222–45.

SATER, JAMES N. 2007. Changing politics from below? Women parliamentarians in Morocco. *Democratization* 14 (4): 723–42.

TAMALE, SYLVIA. 1999. *When Hens Begin to Crow: Gender and Parliamentary Politics in Uganda.* Kampala: Fountain Publishers Ltd.

TRIPP, AILI MARI. 2006. Uganda: agents of change for women's advancement? In *Women in African Parliaments*, edited by Hannah Britton and Gretchen Bauer. Boulder, CO: Lynne Rienner, pp. 111–32.

VINCENT, LOUISE. 2004. Quotas: changing the way things look without changing the way things are. *The Journal of Legislative Studies* 10 (1): 71–96.

WANG, VIBEKE. 2013. Operating in the shadow of the executive: women's substantive representation in the Uganda parliament. PhD dissertation, University of Bergen, Norway.

YOON, MI YOUNG. 2011. More women in the Tanzanian legislature: do numbers matter? *Journal of Contemporary African Studies* 29 (1): 83–98.

ZETTERBERG, PÄR. 2008. The downside of gender quotas? Institutional constraints on women in Mexican state legislatures. *Parliamentary Affairs* 61 (3): 442–60.

ALTERNATIVES TO GENDER QUOTAS: ELECTORAL FINANCING OF WOMEN CANDIDATES IN MALAWI

Happy M. Kayuni and Ragnhild L. Muriaas

Gender quotas change the rules of candidate selection, reflecting a demand-side solution to women's underrepresentation in politics. In contrast, limited attention has been given in the literature to possible supply-side solutions, which would equip women with resources to make them more attractive to selectors—in conjunction with, or separate from, gender quotas. Proposing a new research frontier for quota scholars, this article examines the '50–50 campaign' ahead of the 2009 elections in Malawi, in which donors and the government assisted women aspirants with financial resources and publicity. Although these elections witnessed a 9% rise in women candidates from 2004, some of the increase represented a rise in women running as independents, suggesting that the campaign failed to sufficiently address the role of weak and biased party organisations. While electoral financing can avoid certain disadvantages of gender quotas, it may not be possible to overcome negative perceptions of women in politics.

Introduction

Scholarship on women's representation in advanced democracies has long been concerned with questions about what promotes or hinders women's access to political office and which remedies may be most effective in rapidly increasing women's descriptive representation (Krook 2009; Lawless and Fox 2005; Lawless and Pearson 2008; Norris and Lovenduski 1993). These questions have also been raised in comparative work on democratisation (Bauer and Britton 2006; Lindberg 2004; Muriaas et al. 2013). An influential line of theory uses the economic model of supply and demand to identify factors that may influence recruitment in different political systems (Norris 1993: 310). In a perfect political market the forces of supply and demand would eventually produce equilibrium, as pointed out by Krook (2010: 710), and the proportion of representatives who are women would mirror the proportion of women in the population. This, of course, is seldom the case, as women are underrepresented in almost every national legislature around the world. This implies that there are factors that distort the relationship between the supply of and demand for women representatives.

Supply-side explanations emphasise lack of resources, knowledge and motivation as factors which negatively affect women's access to political office. The representation of women is likely to increase if the pool of eligible women expands, because when women run for political office they tend to win at approximately the same rates as men (Lawless and Pearson 2008: 67). Special schemes designed to equip women with more resources could therefore be a means of increasing women's representation. Demand-side explanations, on the other hand, suggest that the onus for change lies not on women but on political elites

(Krook 2010: 709). Such explanations hold that social bias in legislatures reflects the prejudices of selectors—the party insiders who choose candidates in many political systems—against women (Norris and Lovenduski 1993: 378). Since individual candidates rarely are well known to most selectors, the selectors' judgment of an applicant's abilities, qualifications and experience might be influenced by their perception of the social group that the candidate belongs to (Norris and Lovenduski 1993). The most commonly used demand-side solution to women's underrepresentation is some form of electoral gender quota.

The literature on women's descriptive representation has examined the consequences of three types of gender quotas—voluntary party quotas, legislative quotas and reserved seats—that have been adopted in various countries (Dahlerup 2006; Franceschet et al. 2012; Krook 2009). Less attention has been given to possible supply-side solutions to the underrepresentation of women, with some recent important exceptions, like Krook and Norris (2014). In this study we investigate whether there may be non-quota mechanisms that could be pursued together with, or in lieu of, gender quotas to increase women's political representation. Supply-side solutions include schemes, campaigns and programmes that encourage women to seek political office by equipping them with resources, like money and campaign material. The most prominent of these strategies is to provide electoral financing for women, a mechanism promoted by the United Nations Development Programme (UNDP). According to the UNDP (2007: 6), 'money is a prerequisite for competing in most political systems today', and money and resources are what women most need to compete on an equal footing with men.

Malawi's '50–50 campaign' ahead of the 2009 elections is a critical case to explore whether enlarging the pool of women aspirants through targeted electoral financing leads to more women candidates, and in turn to more women getting elected. At the time of the election, the Malawian government was under intense pressure from the UNDP, the African Union (AU) and the Southern African Development Community (SADC) to reach gender parity in decision-making bodies by 2015. The proportion of women in the national assembly at the time was only 13%,[1] and the government was looking for a plan to fast-track women's representation. Malawi has a majoritarian electoral system, rendering gender quotas potentially problematic or ineffective. Electoral financing, however, appeared to be a feasible option, both financially and politically: it was backed and partly financed by donors, and it did not put the entire burden onto weakly institutionalised political parties. The campaign did not achieve its gender parity goal, but there was a 9.3% increase in women parliamentarians in 2009 to 22.3%. After mapping the campaign and its effects, the article discusses to what extent electoral financing of women can avoid some disadvantages of gender quotas, such as group-specific avenues for representation.

Demand-Side Measures: The Limits of Gender Quotas

During the last two decades governments around the world have found ways to increase the number of women representatives in national legislatures to adhere to national, regional and international laws, treaties and protocols. Gender quotas are the most widely known and extensively researched measure for fast-tracking women's descriptive representation (Dahlerup 2006). Several studies have found that gender quotas have a significant and positive impact on women's numeric representation (Fallon et al. 2012: 392; Paxton et al. 2010: 44; Stockemer 2011: 702; Tripp and Kang 2008: 349). The problem is that certain kinds of gender quotas, such as voluntary party quotas or legal quotas, are less likely to favour the election of women in majoritarian electoral systems than in other systems (Larserud and Taphorn

2007). The most common explanation for why majoritarian electoral systems, characterised by single-member districts, are less likely to foster women candidates is that each district has just one seat. In such cases the nomination becomes a zero-sum game, a situation that is more disadvantageous for women than for men (Matland 1993; Norris 1985; Reynolds 1999; Rule 1981; Tremblay 2012: 7).

Krook et al. (2009: 792) argue that in such institutional settings, 'soft quotas' are often the only remedy that is likely to be implemented. Soft quotas aim to increase women's representation indirectly: they may include internal party quotas or more informal targets in nomination processes. The preference for soft quotas is related not only to the fact that each district has a magnitude of one, but also to the frequent association between majoritarian electoral systems and liberal models of citizenship, favouring equal opportunities over equal results. These models attribute responsibility for unequal outcomes to individuals rather than to structures (Krook et al. 2009: 788); consequently, it is the individuals that need to be 'fixed' and not the rules designed to treat all as equal. For this reason, it is particularly difficult in such systems to secure sufficient political acceptance for rules and laws promoting gender quotas, which may be seen as threatening and unfair by male party members (Zetterberg 2008).

In the literature on women's representation in democratising states, some scholars have noted that legislation often evades these conflicts by adding more seats to the national assemblies and reserving them for women (Muriaas and Wang 2012). This guarantees a certain number of women in national assemblies without diluting the fairness of the competition for mainstream seats. Although reserved seats appear to have the greatest impact on women's representation among the different quota types (Tripp and Kang 2008: 352), they remain controversial. Reserved seats are typically only applied in countries that are classified as nondemocratic by indexes such as Polity IV and Freedom House. Some feminist scholars worry that a system of reserved seats causes tokenism and that women are turned into 'puppet parliamentarians' by powerful executives (Dahlerup 2006: 299). Reserved seats also introduce group-specific avenues of representation that circumvent the existing party system and create new electoral incentives. According to Htun (2004: 442), this is problematic if the ultimate purpose of affirmative action programmes like electoral quotas is to integrate underrepresented groups into existing political institutions. Under such circumstances, the number of reserved seats may become a ceiling, as women are expected to run in their own elections and not interfere in the processes of electing candidates for the mainstream seats (Matland 2006: 287).

Another factor that influences the effects of electoral quotas is party organisation. Highly institutionalised parties rely on rules to achieve their goals, and consequently they are more likely to resort to quotas to increase women's representation (Caul 2001: 1218). However, political parties in democratising states tend to be weakly institutionalised (Randall and Svåsand 2002). In such parties the selection methods are vague, and may change at the whim of party leaders. In Africa, parties rarely represent socioeconomic blocs with different views of state authority; rather, they are primarily vehicles for elite competition (Manning 2005: 715). This means that the selectorate in such parties, the strong party figures who choose candidates, may not have to abide by the rules of the party, as they practically 'own' the party. Consequently, voluntary party quotas, in particular, may be ignored if they are no longer contributing to the popularity of the leadership. Therefore, even if gender quotas have given a strong boost to the descriptive representation of women in some African countries, several circumstances may render such mechanisms less effective. The question is to what extent these measures can be complemented or supplemented with mechanisms aimed at fixing supply-side problems of underrepresentation.

Supply-Side Measures: Electoral Financing

Supply-side instruments to increase women's representation address the resources, and motivations of individuals, unlike demand-side instruments, which manipulate selection rules. The idea is that women who are better equipped to seek political office will not only be more likely to run, but will also be more attractive candidates in the eyes of party selectorates. While there are several types of supply-side instruments, this study focuses on one of the most prominent strategies: targeted electoral financing of women. To provide an overview of its character and potential, we have developed a typology across six dimensions (Table 1). Some of these dimensions are also discussed in the UNDP report *Electoral Financing to Advance Women's Political Participation* (2007).

The variations identified in Table 1 are not mutually exclusive, as real-life programmes may reflect a combination of characteristics—for example, electoral financing may involve both public and private funds, and the pressure for such a scheme may come from both domestic and international sources. The figure does, however, give an idea of how electoral financing of women may vary from context to context. It also helps us put the case selected for this study into comparative perspective.

Electoral financing of women is perceived to be particularly suitable in candidate-centred systems, where the personal financial costs of electioneering tend to be high (Norris 1993: 328). Within candidate-centred systems such as the one in the United States,

Table 1
Typology of variation in gender-based electoral financing

Dimension	Variations	
Recipient	*Parties* A party receives funding if it selects a minimum number of women candidates.	*Women* Funding is provided for all women who register as candidates for elections.
Arrangement	*Direct* Money and campaign material are provided to potential candidates.	*Indirect* Potential candidates benefit from free airtime on television and radio, training workshops, awareness workshops, and assistance in developing networks.
Duration	*Short-term* Assistance is limited to particular elections or election events.	*Long-term* Assistance is provided over the whole election cycle, focusing on supporting the capacity of women parliamentarians, building women's caucuses, and training women leaders.
Source	*Public* The programme is supported by government funding, alone or in combination with other sources.	*Private* Nongovernmental organisations or private firms provide support.
Aim	*Equality of opportunities* All should have the same opportunity to win political office.	*Equality of result* There should be an increase in the number of women in decision-making bodies.
Pressure	*Internal* Domestic groups, inside or outside the political parties, are key actors.	*External* Bilateral and multilateral organisms are key actors.

candidates compete twice: first in the primaries, and then, if they are successful, in elections at the state or national level. To be viable competitors, candidates must raise money, build coalitions of support, create campaign organisations, and develop campaign strategies, all of which may pose greater challenges for women than for men in societies that are historically patriarchal (Lawless and Pearson 2008: 68).

One serious problem with the literature on electoral financing, however, is that most studies focus on the United States. Consequently, it is not clear to what extent these findings are relevant outside the United States as they are based on a context where the only scheme in place is gender-blind public funding for a handful of state legislatures. Seminal studies of women's access to campaign funds in the United States, conducted in the 1980s and 1990s, found that women were no less able than men to raise adequate funds for competitive campaigns (Burrell 1985; Werner 1997: 81). Yet a study by Fox (1997) showed that women perceived fundraising as more difficult than men did. Furthermore, recent studies of public funding programmes in the United States reveal that such schemes did increase the pool of candidates willing and able to run for state legislative offices (Mayer et al. 2006: 247). This suggests that public funding of targeted groups, such as women, could have an impact on women's willingness to run for office.

The Effects of Electoral Financing in Malawi

Although gender quotas have been popular in Africa in recent decades, they seem to have reached a saturation point. In several countries governments and parties have refrained from introducing gender quotas even though intergovernmental organisations, such as the AU and SADC, have tried to bind their members to a gender parity goal. The underrepresentation of women in politics has been seen as a problem that needs to be solved, but in some places gender quotas appear too controversial to be enacted. In Malawi, parties have been encouraged to adopt voluntary gender quotas since the reintroduction of multiparty elections in 1994, but no party has implemented them effectively. By 2004 only two parties had included quota provisions in their political manifestos: the United Democratic Front (UDF) and the Malawi Congress Party (MCP). These provisions, however, were soft quotas, formulated as aims to allocate more seats to women and not as rules to guide selection processes.

The pressure on the government to increase the number of women in parliament intensified after the AU and SADC started to promote gender parity. As the proportion of elected women representatives in the national assembly was only 13% ahead of the 2009 elections, Malawi clearly had a long way to go to reach gender parity by 2015. Instead of adopting gender quotas, however, the government decided to experiment with a different kind of remedy. In collaboration with the donor community, a '50–50 campaign' was launched ahead of the presidential and parliamentary elections scheduled for May 2009. The decision was in line with the UNDP's (2007) promotion of electoral financing; it took into consideration the importance of money in Malawian politics (Lwanda 2006) and the way historical discrimination has curtailed women's economic opportunities (Kanyongolo 2004: 73).

In addition, the campaign did not put all the burden of increasing women's descriptive representation on the political parties. Parties in Malawi are not ideologically distinct; they have weak structures, and each is tightly organised around its founder/leader (Magolowondo and Svåsand 2009). The candidate selection process is fraught with a number of irregularities, as there is often confusion regarding who eligible voters in primaries are as party memberships are unpopular as a consequence of the mandatory party membership law under MCP's authoritarian rule. Such irregularities may, as described below, negatively affect women[2] and in 2009 the candidate selection process in the parties was still a bottleneck in spite of the comprehensive gender parity campaign.

The 50–50 Campaign in the 2009 General Elections

The rationale behind the 50–50 campaign was that many women do not run for elections because it is too expensive. If they run, however, they have the same chances of winning as their male peers. According to UNDP (2007: 11), one of the greatest hurdles a woman faces is financing the process of gaining a nomination; once she is nominated, party support for her may increase and her greater visibility may attract additional sources of funding. Consequently, early money is crucial to the success of women's campaigns. With donor assistance,[3] the 50–50 campaign provided a donation of MK 20 million (US$46,000) ahead of the nomination process. Each female aspirant received a starter pack of MK 100,000 (US$231), and 1000 t-shirts and 2000 posters were produced for each of the 100 female candidates who passed the primary elections (NGOGCN 2009). The NGO Gender Coordination Network (NGOGCN) was established as a permanent, nonpartisan committee to administer the campaign.[4]

The campaign also aimed to sensitise prominent political figures about the importance of increasing women's descriptive representation in the national assembly (MoGCCD 2008). Advocacy meetings with party leadership were organised at the national, regional and district levels, and all six political parties represented in parliament were targeted. In addition, three regional meetings for journalists writing on gender and governance issues were held to stress the importance of reporting on women candidates. The campaign also bought airtime on radio and television to showcase women aspirants. District- and constituency-based sensitisation meetings on women and politics were conducted for community leaders, traditional authorities and religious leaders.

Furthermore, the NGOGCN developed a gender-sensitive toolkit with simple information for voters on the need to cast their vote without gender prejudice (NGOGCN 2009). A total of 140,000 toolkits were produced in different languages, and the task force also distributed stickers, posters, t-shirts and fabric for clothing printed with messages about women and politics. Hence, the campaign not only gave direct financial support to individual women aspirants, but also provided items intended to increase the attractiveness of women candidates in general.

Assessing the Campaign's Success

The success of the campaign in terms of numbers of women candidates and, in the end, the number of women elected to the National Assembly was relatively meagre. At the outset of the campaign there were a total of 400 women aspirants, including those who took part in the primary selection process within their respective political parties as well as independent candidates, according to the Ministry of Gender, Children and Community Development (MoGCCD 2008: 18). Of these, only 239 were certified by the Malawi Electoral Commission as eligible candidates to stand in 144 constituencies in the country. This represented an increase of 83 women from 2004, when 154 women candidates competed for parliamentary seats. It is, however, difficult to say how much the campaign contributed to the 8% increase in women candidates from 2004 to 2009. Since the 1999 elections there has been a steady increase of women candidates from 4 to 12 to 20% of all candidates, suggesting that a rise in women candidates may occur without a comprehensive gender-parity campaign.

Table 2
Contesting candidates by gender and success rate in the 2009 Malawi elections

	Number	% of total	Successful	Success rate (%)
Female	239	20.3	42	17.6
Male	937	79.7	150	16.0
Total	1,176	100.0	192	16.3

Source: Makupe and Namangale (2009).

Some of the increase from 2004 to 2009 represented a rise in the percentage of women running as independents (from 3.6% of all candidates in 2004 to 7.4% in 2009). In the end, only about 13% of the total 1176 candidates in the 2009 elections[5] were women who won the nomination of a political party. The ruling Democratic People's Party (DPP) fielded the most female candidates, as 50 women made it through the DPP nomination process. It thus appears that the 50–50 campaign did not significantly increase the attractiveness of women candidates to the selectorate in the parties. It is likely, however, that the campaign contributed to the 9.3% increase in women parliamentarians in the 2009 general election (from 13% to 22.3% of all MPs). This means that the percentage of women candidates and the percentage of women elected to the national assembly increased by roughly the same amount. The success rate among female contesting candidates was also higher than among male candidates (Table 2).

Among the women candidates, the success rate of the independents was very low: of the 87 female independent candidates, only seven were elected. The success rate was much higher for women candidates who represented political parties (if each political party is independently categorised as a block). This suggests that if women are able to persuade the selectorate to pick them, the electorate will not discriminate against them at the polls.

One way to put the results of the 50–50 campaign into perspective is to compare recent electoral experiences in Malawi with those in Kenya and Zambia, which shared similar features with Malawi in the late 2000s: no history of using instruments to fast-track women's representation, a majoritarian electoral system, a history of competitive elections, and weakly institutionalised political parties. In Kenya, where the 2010 constitution reserved special seats for women, the percentage of women representatives in the national assembly increased from 9.8% to 18.6% from 2007 to 2013. In Zambia, where measures to increase women's numeric representation were not introduced, women's descriptive representation in the national assembly remained flat at about 13.5%. The increase in the proportion of women parliamentarians in Kenya and Malawi, contrasted to the standstill in Zambia, suggests that the introduction of either targeted electoral financing or reserved seats is likely to have had some impact on the number of women representatives. Still, the broader effects of the two different strategies are likely to differ, as discussed below.

Achievements and Challenges to Electoral Financing Strategies

The Malawian strategy of electoral financing of women, we argue, has been slightly more effective in integrating women into existing political institutions than the reserved seats strategy used in Kenya and other African countries such as Rwanda, Tanzania and Uganda. Women parliamentarians in Malawi are not 'add-ons'. The majority of women participating in the 2009 Malawian elections won their candidacies in competition with men, and those who went on to

113

win their elections have clearly defined constituencies. In contrast to women in reserved seats elsewhere, women parliamentarians in Malawi are the single representatives of their constituencies and there is no question about to whom they are responsible. The status of women parliamentarians therefore cannot be questioned. They have won through in a highly candidate-centred system known for its dirty games and weak party organisations.

However, these trends do not necessarily mean that women have gained a strong foothold in the party system in Malawi. Our study of the 2009 elections revealed that none of the parties had clear regulations on how primaries should be conducted. In extreme cases it was not even clear who was eligible to vote, and some candidates were able to capitalise on this confusion to their advantage. There were several reports of financially well-to-do candidates who ferried voters from another constituency to vote for them. Even with financial assistance, most female candidates did not have sufficient resources to engage in such practices. Moreover, women candidates were often disadvantaged because those who were said to be eligible voters—the branch committee members—were predominantly male. Another problem was the fact that the returning officers were generally seasoned party activists who tended to favour their longtime colleagues, whereas women often had not held key positions in their respective parties. A related problem was that even if the parliamentary candidates of the parties were provided with a specific amount for campaigning, those who had been in the party for some time tended to receive extra support. Candidates who had recently joined the party, like most female candidates, did not. The primaries were also frequently marred by threats and violence, and potential female candidates tended to give up the race rather than be intimidated by hired mobs.

The opportunity to run as independent candidates opened up an avenue outside regular party politics, allowing women to run on their own, with support from the government and the donor community. This option clearly was attractive to many Malawian women, given the institutional weakness and bias of the parties. Still, if women are to be integrated into mainstream politics, they cannot focus only on winning as independents.

The 50–50 campaign, as organised in Malawi, also contributed to highlighting the 'differences' that set women candidates apart. Certain features of the campaign led party members and leaders to question the loyalty of the women who were brought forward by the electoral financing scheme. Party figures worried that they might lose influence over their women candidates if the latter adopted the ideologies of the 50–50 campaign. For example, the campaign brought women candidates from rival parties together for training, an initiative usually frowned upon by the party hierarchies. In addition, all parties rejected the campaign cloth provided by the project because it carried only the pictures of the candidates and not party symbols. They pointed out that the 'cloth might confuse voters since there are several women competing in one constituency' (The Nation 2009). The real reason for the rejection of the cloth appeared to be that political parties feared they would not gain an advantage over the competition when only women candidates were featured.

More broadly, some in the parties felt that those behind the 50–50 campaign were pursuing a secret agenda or even colluding with their rivals. Since the campaign was coordinated by the Ministry of Gender, Children, and Community Development, opposition parties questioned the nonpartisanship of the exercise and deemed it to be under the influence of the ruling party. The ruling party, meanwhile, took a suspicious view of the financial resources provided by the campaign. Most of the NGOGCN leaders had been severe critics of government; hence their support of women candidates was regarded as tantamount to support for the opposition, disguised through inclusion of members of the ruling party.

Finally, one election is not sufficient to integrate women into mainstream politics, as it takes time to change party members' attitudes towards female members. Most parties have a women's wing which mobilises women to support the party. In most cases these wings are highly organised, according to interviews with party leaders.[6] It is, however, common to rely on the women's wing mainly for social duties like entertaining the crowd at party meetings. Their influence in the party typically is not felt at top level. As one UDF official stated, 'The women's wing in the party remains the "flower" of the party. They are not rivals in power, rather instruments for the party to achieve its objectives'.[7] Such attitudes must change if women are to be fully integrated into mainstream political structures and make their presence felt.

Implications and Conclusions

Theoretically, electoral financing of women as a supply-side mechanism for increasing women's representation has two clear advantages: first, it is compatible with a majoritarian electoral system, and, second, it does not introduce group-specific avenues of representation that circumvent the existing party system. Women candidates follow the same path to the legislature as men. Additionally, once they are elected, there are no questions as to whom they really represent: women parliamentarians, like their male counterparts, are responsible to their geographically defined constituencies. Still, the outcome of the gender parity campaign in the general elections in Malawi in 2009 would have been meagre if women could run as independents. The option of running as independent candidates in essence created an avenue outside mainstream politics and opened up new electoral incentives. A supply-side mechanism like electoral financing of women has the potential to neutralise the problem of tokenism, but it may not be able to overcome some of the problems connected to the perception of women as 'different' or unsuited to politics.

The study also suggested that in a democratising state like Malawi, where multiparty elections were introduced in 1994, it will take some time before the parties come to regard supply-side mechanisms, like electoral financing of women, as independent of the government. Executives in Uganda, Rwanda and Tanzania have been accused of turning women into puppet parliamentarians with no intention other than to maintain their own rule. It was thus not strange that the Malawian opposition leaders questioned the party loyalty of the women supported by the 50–50 campaign, which was partly financed by the government, had its own agenda, and even produced its own election campaign material. If electoral financing of women is to succeed it should not be organised to show off the good intentions of donors and governments, but designed to enhance the status of women within political parties. It was the political party gatekeepers who had to see women as viable candidates if women are to be integrated into mainstream politics in a sustainable and meaningful way.

NOTES

1. The percentage of women dropped in the third parliament (2004 to 2009) of the current constitution, from 14.6% to 13.0%, as men won more seats than women in by-elections.
2. Interviews with Effie Somanje, independent candidate, 1 February 2009, Blantyre, and Getrude Mkandawire, AFORD (later independent candidate), 5 February 2009, Lilongwe.
3. Key sponsors of the 50/50 programme were the Royal Norwegian Embassy, Canadian International Development Agency (CIDA), Oxfam-GB, UNDP, United Nations Population Fund

(UNFPA), GTZ-MGPDD, ActionAid, DanChurchAid and Netherlands Institute for Multiparty Democracy (NIMD).

4.   The NGOGCN included the Association of Progressive Women (APW), Gender Support Programme (GSP), National Women's Lobby and Rights Group (NWLG), Civil Liberties Committee (CILIC), National Election Systems Trust (NEST), Centre for Human Rights and Rehabilitation (CHRR) and Society for the Advancement of Women (SAW) (NGOGCN 2009: 6).

5.   Compared to 8.6% in 2004 (Khembo 2005: 41).

6.   Interviews with Victoria Chimphonda, Southern Region executive member of the MCP, 17 January 2009, Blantyre; Hophmally Makande, deputy UDF secretary general, 20 February 2009, Blantyre; Juliana Mphande, Southern Region DPP committee member, 28 February 2009, Blantyre; and Elipher Banda, People's Transformation Party (PETRA) committee member, 24 February 2009, Blantyre. (All interviewee affiliations are current as of the date of the interview.)

7.   Interview with Hophmally Makande, deputy UDF secretary general, 20 February 2009, Blantyre.

REFERENCES

BAUER, GRETCHEN and HANNAH E. BRITTON. 2006. Women in African parliaments: a continental shift?. In *Women in African Parliaments*, edited by Gretchen Bauer and Hannah E. Britton. Boulder, CO: Lynne Rienner, pp. 1–30.

BURRELL, BARBARA C. 1985. Women's and men's campaigns for the U.S. House of Representatives, 1972–1982: a finance gap? *American Political Research* 13 (3): 251–72.

CAUL, MIKI. 2001. Women's representation in parliament: the role of political parties. *Party Politics* 5 (1): 79–98.

DAHLERUP, DRUDE (ed.). 2006. *Women, Quotas and Politics*. New York: Routledge.

FALLON, KATHLEEN, LIAM SWISS and JOSELYN VITERNA. 2012. Resolving the democracy paradox: democratization and women's legislative representation in developing nations, 1975 to 2009. *American Sociological Review* 77 (3): 380–408.

FOX, RICHARD L. 1997. *Gender Dynamics in Congressional Elections*. Thousand Oaks, CA: Sage.

FRANCESCHET, SUSAN, MONA LENA KROOK and JENNIFER M. PISCOPO. 2012. Conceptualizing the impact of gender quotas. In *The Impact of Gender Quotas*, edited by Susan Franceschet, Mona Lena Krook and Jennifer M. Piscopo. Oxford: Oxford University Press, pp. 3–25.

HTUN, MALA. 2004. Is gender like ethnicity? The political representation of identity groups. *Perspectives on Politics* 2 (3): 439–58.

KANYONGOLO, FIDELIS EDGE. 2004. The rhetoric of human rights in Malawi: individualization and judicialization. In *Rights and the Politics of Recognition in Malawi*, edited by Harri Englund and Francis B. Nyamnjoh. London: Zed, pp. 64–83.

KHEMBO, NIXON. 2005. Gender and party politics in Malawi. In *Elections and Democratisation in Malawi: An Uncertain Process*, edited by Nixon S. Khembo. Johannesburg: Electoral Institute of Southern Africa (EISA), pp. 40–3.

KROOK, MONA LENA. 2009. *Quotas for Women in Politics: Gender and Candidate Selection Reform Worldwide*. New York: Oxford University Press.

KROOK, MONA LENA. 2010. Beyond supply and demand: a feminist-institutionalist theory of candidate selection. *Political Research Quarterly* 63 (4): 707–20.

KROOK, MONA LENA and PIPPA NORRIS. 2014. Beyond quotas: strategies to promote gender equality in elected office. *Political Studies* 62 (1): 2 20.

KROOK, MONA LENA, JONI LOVENDUSKI and JUDITH SQUIRES. 2009. Gender quotas and models of political citizenship. *British Journal of Political Science* 39 (4): 781–803.

LARSERUD, STINA and RITA TAPHORN. 2007. *Designing for Equality: Best-fit, Medium-fit and Non-favourable Combinations of Electoral Systems and Gender Quotas*. Stockholm: International Institute for Democracy and Electoral Assistance (International IDEA).

LAWLESS, JENNIFER L. and RICHARD L. FOX. 2005. *It Takes a Candidate: Why Women Don't Run for Office*. Cambridge: Cambridge University Press.

LAWLESS, JENNIFER and KATHRYN PEARSON. 2008. The primary reason for women's underrepresentation? Reevaluating the conventional wisdom. *Journal of Politics* 70 (1): 67–82.

LINDBERG, STAFFAN I. 2004. Women's empowerment and democratization: the effects of electoral systems, participation, and experience in Africa. *Studies in Comparative International Development* 39 (1): 28–53.

LWANDA, JOHN. 2006. Kwacha: the violence of money in Malawi's politics. *Journal of Southern African Studies* 32 (3): 525–44.

MAGOLOWONDO, AUGUSTINE and LARS SVÅSAND. 2009. One man ownership: political parties and their struggle for democratic standards. In *Democracy in Process: Malawi's 2009 Parliamentary and Presidential Elections*, edited by Martin Ott and Fidelis Edge Kanyongolo. Zomba, Malawi: Kachere, pp. 265–94.

MAKUPE, CECILIA and JIMMY NAMANGALE. 2009. Statistical figures and facts: the results of Malawi's 2009 presidential and parliamentary elections. In *Democracy in Process: Malawi's 2009 Parliamentary and Presidential Elections*, edited by Martin Ott and Fidelis Edge Kanyongolo. Zomba, Malawi: Kachere, pp. 295–311.

MANNING, CARRIE. 2005. African party systems after the third wave. *Party Politics* 11 (6): 707–27.

MATLAND, RICHARD. 1993. Institutional variables affecting female representation in national legislatures: the case of Norway. *Journal of Politics* 55 (3): 737–55.

MATLAND, RICHARD. 2006. Electoral quotas: frequencies and effectiveness. In *Women, Quotas and Politics*, edited by Drude Dahlerup. New York: Routledge, pp. 275–92.

MAYER, KENNETH R., TIMOTHY WERNER and AMANDA WILLIAMS. 2006. Do public funding programs enhance electoral competition? In *The Marketplace of Democracy: Electoral Competition and American Politics*, edited by Michael McDonald and John Samples. Washington, DC: Brookings Institution Press, pp. 245–67.

MOGCCD (MINISTRY OF GENDER, CHILDREN AND COMMUNITY DEVELOPMENT). 2008. *Women and Political Participation in the 2009 Parliamentary and Presidential Elections*. Lilongwe: MOGCCD.

MURIAAS, RAGNHILD L. and VIBEKE WANG. 2012. Executive dominance and the politics of quota representation in Uganda. *Journal of Modern African Studies* 50 (2): 309–38.

MURIAAS, RAGNHILD L., LIV TØNNESSEN and VIBEKE WANG. 2013. Exploring the relationship between democratization and quota policies in Africa. *Women's Studies International Forum* 41, part 2: 89–93.

THE NATION. 2009. Parties reject 50–50 gender campaign cloth, 6 February, p. 2.

NGOGCN (NGO GENDER COORDINATION NETWORK). 2009. *NGOGCN Institutional Profile*. Lilongwe. Available at http://www.ngogcn.org.mw/images/PDF/Updated%20NGOCGN%20Institutional%20profile.pdf, accessed 10 July 2013.

NORRIS, PIPPA. 1985. Women's legislative participation in western Europe. *West European Politics* 8 (4): 90–101.

NORRIS, PIPPA. 1993. Conclusions: comparing legislative recruitment. In *Gender and Party Politics*, edited by Joni Loveduski and Pippa Norris. London: Sage, pp. 309–30.

NORRIS, PIPPA and JONI LOVENDUSKI. 1993. 'If only more candidates came forward': supply-side explanations of candidate selection in Britain. *British Journal of Political Science* 23 (3): 373–408.

PAXTON, PAMELA, MELANIE HUGHES and MATTHEW PAINTER. 2010. Growth in women's political representation: a longitudinal exploration of democracy, electoral system and gender quotas. *European Journal of Political Research* 49 (1): 25–52.

RANDALL, VICKY and LARS SVÅSAND. 2002. Party institutionalization in new democracies. *Party Politics* 8 (1): 5–29.

REYNOLDS, ANDREW. 1999. Women in the legislatures and executives of the world: knocking at the highest glass ceiling. *World Politics* 51 (4): 547–72.

RULE, WILMA. 1981. Why women don't run: the critical contextual factors in women's legislative recruitment. *Political Research Quarterly* 34 (1): 60–77.

STOCKEMER, DANIEL. 2011. Women's parliamentary representation in Africa: the impact of democracy and corruption on the number of female deputies in national parliaments. *Political Studies* 59 (3): 693–712.

TREMBLAY, MANON. 2012. Introduction. In *Women and Legislative Representation: Electoral Systems, Political Parties and Sex Quotas*, edited by Manon Tremblay. New York: Palgrave Macmillan.

TRIPP, AILI MARI and ALICE KANG. 2008. The global impact of quotas: on the fast track to increased female legislative representation. *Comparative Political Studies* 41 (3): 338–61.

UNDP (UNITED NATIONS DEVELOPMENT PROGRAMME). 2007. *Electoral Financing to Advance Women's Political Participation: A Guide for UNDP Support.* New York: UNDP.

WERNER, BRIAN L. 1997. Financing the campaigns of women candidates and their opponents. *Women and Politics* 18 (1): 81–97.

ZETTERBERG, PÄR. 2008. The downside of gender quotas? Institutional constraints on women in Mexican state legislatures. *Parliamentary Affairs* 61 (3): 442–60.

Index